The Potemkin Mutiny

The battleship *Potemkin* at anchor at Constanza

The torpedo boat №267, unwilling accomplice in the mutiny, just before leaving Constanza for the last time

The Potemkin Mutiny

BY

RICHARD HOUGH

Illustrated

SEVERN HOUSE PUBLISHERS

First published in Great Britain, 1960, by Hamish Hamilton Ltd
This 1975 edition from Severn House Publishers

ISBN 0 7278 0045 0

Printed in Great Britain by Flarepath Printers Ltd,
St Albans, Herts and bound by Wm Brendon & Son Ltd,
Tiptree, Essex

CONTENTS

ILLUSTRATIONS

Preface

TIME, and propaganda, have so clouded the truth of the *Potemkin* mutiny that it must surely be among the most inaccurately recorded events in naval history. Present Russian accounts, and even descriptions of the event written by the same eye-witness on different occasions, are at variance in detail; and none of these tally precisely with those of officers of the Black Sea Fleet who are alive today. The chief difficulty is that, although it took place only 55 years ago, it has already attained legendary status in the U.S.S.R., with the battleship as a sacred memorial and Afanasy Matushenko as a revered martyr of the 1905 revolution. To émigré Russian officers memories of the incident are naturally coloured in some degree by shame and indignation; and it is as foolish to expect the Soviet version to be any more accurate than a Tudor rendering of the Battle of Bosworth.

There is no dispute on the main events, and their sequence. Where there are conflicting reports I have done my best to reconcile them, and, where necessary, to keep a reasonable balance between supposition and probability, relying where possible on what is known of the character of the participants. As an extreme example, where the official contemporary account makes no mention of the tarpaulin incident, officers have always denied that there was even any threat of shooting the leading mutineers, and all the sailors, as well as the official Soviet histories, being emphatic that the men were covered by a tarpaulin, I have concluded that

Commander Giliarovsky, in an attempt to bluff the men into submission, found himself in a hopeless postion and ordered the squad to open fire in a panic. This seems to me the most reasonable interpretation.

The most useful sources have been the detailed reports written by Afanasy Matushenko and Constantine Feldmann, and accounts of the mutiny by Robert L. Hadfield, Tom Wintringham, Irving Anthony, and the admirable article by Captain Geoffrey Bennett, R.N., (retd.) published recently in the Journal of the R.U.S.I. Consular Despatches from Odessa and the private diary of the British Consul-General were also invaluable in checking times and some doubtful details.

I should like to thank the members of the American Society for Russian Naval History; the Association of Imperial Russian Naval Officers in America; Miss Helen Romanova, Vice-Chairman of the Foreign Commission Union of Writers of the U.S.S.R.; and the Historical Institute of the Academy of Science of the U.S.S.R., for providing me with information. I owe a special debt to Commander George Taube, R.I.N., of New York, for the time he gave to answering my queries and to writing to fellow officers of the Russian Imperial Navy.

May 1960   RICHARD HOUGH

CHAPTER I

A Matter of Maggots

W HAT were a few maggots? It was excellent meat. The ship's senior surgeon, Honourable Counsellor Smirnov, had pronounced it of first quality. There was, he said, no justification for the complaints.

The disturbance which had begun as a murmur at dawn, circulating gently, had then spread and grown in volume and bitterness. Like oilmen at a gusher, the ship's agitators had risen to the occasion and fought to tame these sudden riches to their purpose. It had been their busiest morning since the November uprising at Sevastopol, and by the time the dinner gongs were sounding at mid-day, they had succeeded in creating an atmosphere of threatening purpose. Mutiny was in the air, bearing down on the battleship *Potemkin* with the inevitability of a predicted typhoon.

* * * *

Until that morning of June 27, 1905, Captain Eugene N. Golikov of the *Potemkin* had every reason to be satisfied with the state of morale in his ship. Compared with many others in the Black Sea Fleet, his crew had seemed free of strong revolutionary elements, and there had been no trouble ashore during the period of the refit she had just completed at Sevastopol. Vice-Admiral Krieger, temporarily commanding in the absence of Admiral Chukhnin, must also have felt confident of the *Potemkin's* loyalty to have detached her at a time when reports of increasing seditious activity were reaching him from every battleship in the Fleet. On June 25, Captain Golikov received orders to sail to Tendra Strait to test the new linings of his 12-inch and 6-inch guns before the main manoeuvres began. Shortly before mid-day the great battleship, newly painted black with deep yellow upperworks and black-banded funnels, left the Black Sea Fleet's main base and steered north-west for her destination, 150 miles away. Golikov's wife was to follow in the naval transport *Viekha* in order to be near her husband during the period of the manoeuvres, when he hoped to spend several nights ashore in the town.

The voyage was uneventful, but when the *Potemkin* dropped anchor early on June 26 in Tendra Bay, a few miles off the long, deserted strip of Tendra Island, the sea was too choppy and the wind too fresh for the test firings to be carried out successfully, although the temperature remained high. In the early afternoon, Golikov made a signal to his accompanying 100-ton torpedo-boat, commanded by Lieutenant Baron Klodt von Jurgensburg, ordering him to Odessa to purchase provisions from the marine butchers and grocers in the harbour area of the town. It seemed a sensible way of filling in the time and would make the N267 available all the next day for target practice duties, if the weather permitted. In the evening N267 returned with sacks of flour, groceries, wine and delicacies for the *Potemkin's* wardroom. Spread in a row across her little deck were the big carcasses of beef which were destined for the *Potemkin's* cauldrons to be made into the crew's staple diet of meat *bortsch*. There was enough of it to last the cooks until the ship was joined by the rest of the Black Sea Fleet for the summer manoeuvres, due to start on July 4. Later in the evening the meat was hoisted aboard the battleship and hung up on the spar deck from hooks. If decay had already set in, on that evening it was too dark for anyone to observe it; and it was not until the following morning that the attention of a sailor on the four-to-eight watch swabbing down the spar deck was drawn to the carcasses by their evil smell. On closer inspection he saw that the meat was riddled with white maggots, and that they were active. Perhaps it had been high before it had been purchased in Odessa, or exposure to the heat, exceptional even for the Black Sea in June, may have caused it to go off. Within minutes a small group of men, carrying buckets and swabs and with their sleeves and bell-bottoms rolled up, were standing round the obscene swinging objects. The crowd grew as the word spread down to the crew's quarters and to the mess decks, where the forenoon watch was breakfasting off black bread and tea. When the watches changed there were more than a hundred men in an unorganised protest demonstration, humming with indignation and pushing one another in order to get a close look at the squirming maggots.

The men were shouting their protests when one of the 'conductors' or petty officers, hurried along to investigate, and he could recognise certain voices raised above the others among the cries of "It's not fit for pigs," "Let's get the doctor to look at it," "Chuck the stinking stuff overboard." It was evident that the agitators were already hard at work. The men fell back hesitantly at the petty officer's orders, like the big blue flies that had come with the morning sun; but only hovered ready to return with their courage. "All right, but call the doctor," a voice cried out from the back, "even the Japanese wouldn't feed us with stuff like this."

*   *   *   *

When news of his crew's disaffection reached Captain Golikov later on the morning of June 27, it is unlikely that he was greatly alarmed. By the standards of the Imperial Russian Navy, and in contrast with his second-in-command and many of his own junior officers, he was a tolerant and even lax commander; and complaints about the food were, after all, common enough in the service. There was no real cause for anxiety yet. From his cabin aft in the *Potemkin* he sent a message to his senior surgeon asking him to inspect the carcasses and to report their condition to him.

Surgeon Smirnov, a tall, narrow-faced officer dressed in his full-length coat, carrying the three black stars of his rank on his silver epaulettes, left the wardroom at once and proceeded, accompanied by a petty officer, forward to the spar deck, where a small group of sailors was still gathered. This hard core had refused to disperse, and had already witnessed the arrival and departure of the ship's butchers with sufficient meat for that day's dinner. Smirnov recognised the attitude of unusual defiance and insubordination in the men by the manner in which they glanced at him and only reluctantly allowed him to break through.

"Now what's all this about—what's all this about?" Smirnov demanded of them. He covered what must have been the first traces of fear by bustling officiously and talking loudly as he slipped on his pince-nez and bent down to look at the carcasses. His examination was brief and cursory. "It's excellent meat," he told the petty officer. "Nothing wrong with it. Just a wash with some vinegar, that's all it needs." And he pushed past the men again to report this satisfactory and reassuring news to his captain.

So far as Captain Golikov was concerned the incident was over: it had been no more than a minor flare-up, of the kind that had become unhappily frequent in a fleet cut off from the Far East fighting, and demoralised by the news of the defeats in Manchuria and the almost total destruction of the rest of the Imperial Navy. At the same time the men were acutely aware of the great social upheavals that were occurring all over the Empire, from Warsaw to Vladivostock, St Petersburg to the Crimea. The weather seemed to be easing, Captain Golikov noticed; with any luck he would be able to order out the torpedo-boat with the targets in the afternoon and they would be able to begin the gunnery tests. His wife was due at Odessa the following evening, and he hoped to have completed the exercise by then so that he would be able to join her. As a precautionary measure, for Surgeon Smirnov had indicated that the men had shown unusual insubordination, he ordered a sentry to be posted on the spar deck with a pencil and paper to take the name of any man who approached the meat. They were easily enough scared, these peasant conscripts, and he was confident that this measure would prevent further trouble.

By mid-day, the wind had died, the sea was calm and the sun beat down almost vertically on the empty decks of the battleship. The *Potemkin*, brilliant in her paintwork, as spotless and as outwardly placid as if prepared for a royal review, seemed far removed from acts of violence. There was only one officer aboard who continued to feel concern about the state of unrest of the men. He was Commander Ippolit Giliarovsky, the tough, uncompromising disciplinarian and second-in-command; a young and handsome aristocrat who was the most feared and hated officer in the ship. Giliarovsky made it his business to be more closely acquainted with the real state of morale of the ship's crew than his captain, both by frequent inspections and by regular consultations with certain of the most trusted petty officers. Word had already reached his ears that a dangerous change had come over the men, that the trouble-makers aboard the ship had succeeded in converting at least temporarily to the cause of the revolution, many previously un-committed crew members. Where pamphlets and per-suasion had failed in the weeks past, some stinking carcasses were succeeding.

While his fellow officers answered the 'dine-and-wine' call from the wardroom, Giliarovsky made a sudden escorted tour of the mess decks forward to make sure that his anxieties were without foundation. He at once found the men more uneasy and threatening even than he had feared. The place was in a state of uproar, sailors shout-ing their defiance and beating their eating irons on the mess tables. It appeared as if a major riot might break out at any moment. The cauldrons of meat *bortsch* were steaming and ready in the ship's *caboose*, or galley, but not one among the six hundred or so men present was eating it. Giliarovsky, still unnoticed by all but a few men, walked rapidly over to the open serving hatches and demanded to know what was going on and why the men were not eating.

"They won't touch their *bortsch*, sir," he was told by Ivan Daniluc, one of the cooks. "They said we ought to throw it overboard—and the rest of the meat as well." He pointed to the nearest table. "You see, sir, they're only eating their bread and water, though they've asked us for tea and butter."

Giliarovsky turned angrily on the men nearest the hatches, who had now quietened down under the threat of his proximity, and attempted to make his voice heard above the cries from the rest of the crew. "Silence, do you hear?" he shouted. "What do you think you're doing? This is a disgraceful demonstration. Why don't you eat your *bortsch*?"

Half lost in the confusion of shouts and jeers, Giliarov-sky could just make out one or two broken sentences: "Because the meat is stinking!" "Eat it yourself—we'll stick to bread and water."

Seeing that conditions were now out of hand, and being anxious to avoid further humiliation, Giliarovsky departed to consult his captain. But on his way, he paused in the wardroom behind Surgeon Smirnov's chair and said to him quietly, to avoid creating alarm among the others, "Mr Smirnov, the crew are refusing to eat their soup. They say it's bad. Do you know anything about this?"

"Of course," the surgeon answered crossly, "I have already examined it and said that the meat brought yesterday is excellent. The maggots are nothing but eggs which the flies have laid. They're easily washed off with vinegar and water."

"Thank you, Mr Smirnov."

The pace of events on the *Potemkin* was now rapidly increasing as more and more among both the officers and men became aware that a crisis was at hand, and acted accordingly. Giliarovsky interrupted Captain Golikov's luncheon, which he was taking in his cabin, and reported on the situation. "Something will have to be done, sir, right away," he told him urgently.

Golikov agreed, but as a naturally cautious man, he was not in favour of too hasty action and rang for a messenger and told him to ask both the chief surgeon and his assistant, Dr Golenko, to report to him at once. Golikov liked to be certain of his facts before finally making a decision. Asked to confirm once again that the meat was fresh and that there was no justification for the men's refusal to eat it, Smirnov had difficulty in controlling his patience. He did not care for his word to be doubted.

"Very well, doctor, and thank you," the ship's captain said. "Commander Giliarovsky, will you please order the drums to be beaten for roll-call on the quarterdeck."

It was one o'clock and time for the afternoon watch to take over, when Captain Eugene Golikov left his cabin for the last time as commander of his ship, and made his way up to the quarterdeck with the officer-of-the-watch, Junior Lieutenant Alexeev, and Commander Giliarovsky. The entire ship's company of some 670 men, with the exception of the other officers who remained in the wardroom, was already assembled in line upon line aft and along both sides of the stern 12-inch gun turret. They were dressed in their summer uniform of white bell-bottoms, white jumper over blue-and-white striped jersey, and cap with long ribbon-tail falling down the back. They looked neat and clean, and but for their moustaches, the Slavic set of their dark features, and short stature, might almost have been the crew of a Royal Navy battleship on the Mediterranean station awaiting inspection.

They also appeared to have lost entirely their spirit of sedition at the prospect of a general dressing-down from their captain, and their silence and orderly appearance must have reassured Golikov in his confidence in their loyalty as he passed through the gap in the ranks left for him. He was a heavily built man, and he mounted the capstan in the centre of the quarterdeck with some difficulty.

From his superior height, Captain Golikov glanced over the close-packed ranks, line upon line covering the entire quarterdeck, a subdued sea of bobbing white caps against the blue sea and the dead black of the 12-inch gun turret. He was well aware that there was hardly a real seaman among them. Except for the bo'suns and petty officers and a few long-service men, they were nearly all conscripts, totally illiterate and crude in their habits, men who had never got their feet wet and who would still be doubled over the soil in Bessarabia or the Ukraine but for the Far East war. They should be treated, he considered, sternly, but simply, more as recalcitrant children than as dangerous insurrectionists.

"We have repeatedly told you," he began in a strong voice, "that disorders like these are utterly forbidden in a warship of the Imperial Navy. You don't appear to understand that for stirring up a demonstration you can be strung up on the yard-arm." And he pointed up to the mast to underline his threat. "Honourable Counsellor Smirnov, our senior surgeon, has examined the meat you have complained about, and assures me that the quality is excellent. Now, men, let us have no more of this nonsense. Whoever is willing to eat the *bortsch*, step forward two paces."

For a moment there was silence and not a man moved. Then slowly, as if impelled forward, a number of the petty officers and bo'suns and a few of the older men, broke ranks. But none followed, and suddenly the silence on the quarterdeck had become more dangerously threatening even than the tumult on the mess deck earlier.

"Very well, then," called out Golikov with finality, as if about to act on his threat, "if you won't eat your *bortsch*, there is nothing else for it. I shall seal some of the meat in a bottle for the analysts and report the whole matter to the Commander-in-Chief. He shall decide what shall be done with you. You are dismissed." The captain climbed down from the capstan and without another word or a glance at his men, hurried off back to his cabin as if fearing pursuit, Lieutenant Alexeev following at his heels.

The ringleaders could not have asked for a more complete capitulation. But if they were surprised and even caught off their guard by this sudden turn of events, Commander Giliarovsky was horrified. After this victory he knew that the men would be quite uncontrollable and the state of the ship must become anarchic.

What could have come over the captain to treat them so leniently? Giliarovsky decided to take the initiative at once before everything was lost. Leaping onto the capstan even before Golikov was out of sight, he called out, "Reform ranks—at attention! Bo'sun, call out the guard—and bring a tarpaulin."

Only a few among the older men, and the corporals and petty officers and warrant officers, understood the possible significance of this order. Under old naval disciplinary practice, now long superseded, a ship's commander would call out a firing squad, and to preserve as far as possible the impersonal element to the proceedings, order a sail-cloth to be thrown over mutineers before having them shot. Furious as he was, it is unlikely that Giliarovsky had any intention of acting on the implied threat behind his order. Discipline in the Imperial Navy was no more and no less severe than in the Royal Navy, and if rather more individual latitude was allowed to senior officers—in the way of flogging, for example—Giliarovsky knew that he was limited to ordering a seaman fifteen lashes or a month's imprisonment, and that if he exceeded his powers he would be in serious trouble.

Commander Giliarovsky was bluffing, there seems little doubt of that, and the first response among the men after the order had been barked out so loudly that none could fail to hear it, appeared to justify the bluff. Rapidly the word spread round, circulating like ripples from the men who knew that a tarpaulin meant death by shooting, that the ringleaders would soon be facing the firing squad. From amidships came the steady hammer-beat of a marching squad; and preceding them came eight corporals in peaked caps carrying at a half trot the heavy tarpaulin. Giliarovsky, tall, imposing and threatening, stared impassively over the heads of the men and awaited from the capstan the arrival of the firing squad. This action he was taking on his own initiative might be drastic and even dangerous, but he was confident of its efficacy.

It was men like Afanasy Matushenko, Fyodor Mikishkin and Josef Dymtchenko who had been working all morning to create purpose and direction from the disaffection on the lower decks. Torpedo quartermaster Matushenko was the supreme revolutionary commander and official Social-Democrat leader in the *Potemkin*, a short, sturdy, vigorous-looking man, with high Slavic cheekbones and with the intent glitter of the zealot in his little dark eyes. There was not a man on the battleship's lower decks who had not witnessed or surrendered to Matushenko's powers of persuasion; and though many might be weary of his continued hectoring and pamphleteering, and others were afraid of his consciousness of power and fanaticism, he was widely respected and recognised as a man of great courage and daring. The converted would, Matushenko knew, follow him anywhere; the rest would follow behind like the simple peasants they were.

Matushenko and his lieutenants now suddenly recognised that the moment had come to touch off the charge that had so fortuitously been laid to their fuse. First the high meat and the surgeon's refusal to condemn it; and now this unexpected threat of violence. If the officers had set out to conspire their own destruction, they could hardly have arranged events more conveniently. Matushenko had only to calculate the moment to strike, and that moment was fast approaching.

The guard of twelve men, in blue jumpers and trousers and armed with bayonetted rifles, arrived on the quarter-deck in two columns, led by a bo'sun, and were lined up facing aft with their backs to the ship's crew, and directly in front of the commander. Giliarovsky glanced down at them, and then over their heads to the men beyond, whose restlessness was in such contrast to the guards' immobility.

"Now we'll try again," began Giliarovsky, seemingly oblivious to the obsessed, ominous air that now hung over the crew as he awaited their decision. "All those prepared to eat the *bortsch*, step forward."

Again there was a moment of uncertainty, and again the almost apologetic step forward by the older men. Giliarovsky waited, still confident that the presence of the armed guard would this time turn the tide. A few more followed, but not more than fifty in all. His patience was fast draining away, faster than the courage of the men.

"So it's mutiny, is it?" he called out angrily at last. "All right, we know how to deal with that. If you think there is no discipline in the Navy, then I'll show you how wrong you are. Bo'sun, bring the ringleaders here."

With two members of the guard, the bo'sun walked boldly into the tight ranks, arbitrarily selecting a man here, a man there, who was dragged away by the guard until a dozen seamen were grouped in an untidy huddle by the rails.

"Now throw the tarpaulin over them," he ordered the corporals who had been standing by. "And we'll see what the other mutineers have to say." Once again he turned back to the men, and at this third appeal there was an unmistakable note of hysteria in his voice. "Those who will eat their *bortsch* are dismissed, anyone who remains can see for himself what we do with mutineers in the Navy."

It will never be known whether, at this point, the *Potemkin's* first officer suddenly recognised that his bluff had been called and that he was committed to ordering the squad to fire, or whether he realised that, like his captain, he would be obliged finally to capitulate. But if he was gripped by uncertainty, the period of agonised indecision was brief. From the rear of the starboard section of men Afanasy Matushenko, was edging his way forward, speaking quietly to the men he passed. The other ringleaders followed his example, like beaters edging through standing corn, and the agitation that followed in their train broke up the final semblance of symmetry in the ranks. Ahead was the double line of sailors, at their side the rifles brilliantly-silvered where the sun caught the bayonet blades; beyond stood the manifestation of their fear, sword hanging low at his side, the stars of his rank clear on his shoulders; and beyond again, huddled and poignant beneath the tarpaulin and with only their shuffling feet visible, were the men awaiting execution.

An urgent exchange of words appeared to be taking place between Giliarovsky and Midshipman Liventzov, who had been standing alongside and below the commander since he had sprung on to the capstan. To the watching men it seemed that the moment of decision had come, and that Giliarovsky was instructing the midshipmen to pass on the order to fire to the petty officer in command of the squad.

Matushenko now forced his way towards the front ranks with increased determination, pushing the men aside and calling out to the members of the firing squad, "Don't shoot your own comrades—you can't kill your own shipmates! Don't fire, comrades!" The appeal rapidly spread, voice rising above voice.

"Get yourselves rifles and ammunition," came the cries, "we're taking over the ship."

With those words, full scale mutiny had been irrevocably invoked, and nothing could save the *Potemkin* and her officers. The undecided were caught up in the sudden flood tide, and even those who were to remain loyal in spirit to authority were swept along. Some seven hundred men were running amok, and nothing but a fusillade could have quelled them.

In those agonised seconds, Commander Giliarovsky must have been well aware of this, and whatever his earlier intentions may have been, now he shouted directly at the squad to open fire. Like his captain, he had a low opinion of the courage of the men and was confident that the sound of shots alone could break the uprising. But he had underestimated the powers of leadership the ringleaders had acquired. The men were already beyond control, many were racing towards the spar deck and the armoury. The squad was resolute only in its refusal to raise its rifles, more fearful of the wrath of the mob than of the unarmed officer still futilely ordering them to shoot.

Now desperate, Giliarovsky leapt down from the capstan and wrenched a rifle from the nearest man. "So you're in on this, too, are you?" he called out to the rest of the bluejackets furiously. "You obey orders or——" At that moment the first shot rang out, the first bullet sang overhead.

Like any warship, the *Potemkin* had known only order governed by a strict code of discipline since she had first been commissioned five years before. In no other circumstances is insurrection so sharp in its application, and the contrast between restraint and anarchy so appalling in its impact, as on a man-o'-war in peace-time, when hundreds of men live packed in their steel shell for no other purpose than to conform to the strict routine of their existence. In the *Potemkin* the situation was irritated even further by the hot spirit of revolution that was then infusing the whole nation and whose spirit of hate and despair had found its way down to the lower decks of every vessel in the Black Sea Fleet. No other mutiny in history can have flared up so quickly into flames so searing and uncontrollable as the mutiny in the battleship *Potemkin*.

Able Seaman Gregori Vakulinchuk was the first to return from the armoury, where the rifles stood pyramid-stacked, to the aft end of the gundeck. It had been a frenzied race involving only the most determined of the men, while many more hovered uncertainly or ran and shouted without purpose, aware only of the confusion that reigned without obvious cause all about them and only intuitively recognising that self-survival depended on remaining neutral for the present.

Vakulinchuk had fired that first shot, but it might have been from a starter's pistol fired high only for effect. Giliarovsky ran to meet him, shooting with hasty aim and without effect twice across the quarterdeck, and closed with the mutineer near the 12-inch gun turret hatch. Vakulinchuk tried to bring his rifle to bear on the officer, but Giliarovsky got his shot in first, and Vakulinchuk crumpled up half in and half out of the turret.

Afanasy Matushenko was at the head of a group of armed seamen who came off the spar deck at that moment. He saw the wounded man lying at Giliarovsky's feet. He saw Giliarvosky swing his rifle round, take aim, and fire twice, missing both times; and then heard him calling out, "Drop your rifle—do you hear? Drop your rifle."

"You'll have to kill me first," Matushenko replied. "Get off the ship, it belongs to us now."

Again Giliarovsky raised his rifle, but Matushenko was too quick for him. A single shot rang out and the *Potemkin's* first officer fell dead to the deck.

The remainder of the armed men, some fifty in all, had not paused in their charge on to the quarterdeck. Midshipman Liventzov, who had remained beside the capstan, confused and undecided, watched in horror Vakulinchuk's exchange of shots with Giliarovsky and the arrival of the mob of armed men led by Matushenko. Liventzov, too, attempted to snatch at a rifle from one of the members of the firing squad to support his senior officer. But he was too late. There was no longer any indecision among the bluejackets and he was thrown aside, to be shot down by a volley of bullets within seconds of Giliarovsky's death.

The next to die was the Gunnery Officer, Lieutenant Neoupokoev, who rashly came up on to deck from the wardroom, where news of the mutiny had arrived only with the sound of the first gunshots. Matushenko was the first to spot him and at once raised his rifle and fired. The shot fell low, ricocheting off the deck, and Neoupokoev leaped into the air in spontaneous reaction to the near miss.

"Try that again," a voice called out. Several men were laughing uncontrollably and firing their rifles into the air for lack of a target. As Neoupokoev turned to run for cover, Matushenko fired again, then twice more, deliberately aiming at the lieutenant's feet this time, so that he was forced to leap high off the deck in fear. Then, as if tiring of the sport, Matushenko took more careful aim and shot him dead. "Over the side with him," he ordered. It was time to organise the mutiny, to drive out from cover the other officers and take formal control of the battleship.

To the great mass of previously uncommitted sailors their future course of action was now clear. Violence had come suddenly, bewilderingly and dangerously from two sides; but there could no longer be any doubt which side would ultimately triumph. Like boys responding to the call of a playground bully, they struggled to get at the sprawled bodies to hurl them over the rails, and cheered derisively as they splashed into the sea below. Many more now had rifles and pistols from the armoury and were keen to find targets at which to fire. This would not be difficult, for there had been eighteen officers beside the captain in the ship, every one of them somewhere still aboard.

"Come on, comrades, hunt them down," a voice was urging them from the top of the big gun turret. "The ship's not ours yet." And at once the blooded pack was off in full cry, spreading out on the main deck, the spar deck, and the gun deck, down gangways to the lower compartments of the ship, and aft to the wardroom and officers' quarters. They made a tremendous noise as they ran along the steel decks, wrenched open and s̲l̲a̲m̲m̲e̲d shut steel hatches and doors, and shouted at the tops of their voices. Even the less enthusiastic and politically ignorant were shouting slogans about freedom and vengeance and death to the tyrants. It seemed as if the whole ship's company was intoxicated by the release from tension and the shock of sudden murder, and could find expression only in more and more noise, and more killing.

Someone caught a glimpse of Junior Lieutenant Vakhtin emerging from his cabin and at once opened fire. More shots followed, and there was renewed shouting as a group of men pursued him up on to the main deck, then to the upper deck, where he was twice hit by bullets before he succeeded in reaching the rails and throwing himself overboard. Other officers followed him into the sea, and for some minutes there occurred the extraordinary spectacle of hatless officers of the Imperial Navy emerging at intervals like rabbits from a ferret-ridden warren, on to the *Potemkin's* main and upper decks, and racing for the greater safety of the water below. Each was followed by a shouting mob, of greater or lesser number, firing wildly at the target when he could be seen, and often when he could not. Several armed men took up positions at strategic points on the upper deck, firing on the officers in the brief moment of their flight to the rails and overboard, while others hung about closer to the side of the ship and took more leisurely shots as they swam away.

Some escaping officers were lucky and ran the gauntlet of fire and pursuit from the wardroom to the deck, into the sea and beyond rifle range without being touched. Paymaster Lieutenant Makarov and the Engineer Officers Nazarov and Zaouskevitch were among these. A junior lieutenant got safely into the water and was heading strongly for the torpedo boat N267 when a bullet struck him. This water target-practice was proving more and more popular as opportunities increased and as the helplessness of the victims, fully clothed and in a sea that was still choppy for swimmers, became apparent. Lieutenant Grigoriev disappeared under a hail of bullets and did not surface again. He was only on temporary assignment to the *Potemkin* and could not have been the subject of any special grievance. There was no longer interest in the identity of any officer; during those wild minutes the evidence of commissioned rank alone was sufficient justification for murder. But in the hysterical excitement and pandemonium that had seized the men, six more officers succeeded in throwing themselves overboard and swimming beyond range and alongside the torpedo-boat unharmed.

*　　*　　*　　*

One man alone among the officers of the *Potemkin* made any attempt to stem the tide of mutiny after the death of Giliarovsky. He was the ship's Torpedo Officer, Lieutenant Wilhelm C. Tonn, a young man who had always been regarded with fear and respect and as a strict disciplinarian by the sailors. He appeared suddenly on the quarterdeck when the pandemonium and the killing were at their height; and to defy the mutineers at this stage required courage of a remarkable order. His revolver was drawn, and he revealed at once in his demeanour that he had no intention of fleeing. Several men caught sight of him from the gun deck above, and fired their rifles and revolvers at him; but he stayed his ground, untouched by the gunfire and calling out, "Drop your weapons, you fools—you'll all be shot for this." Momentarily taken aback by this attitude of defiance, the shooting ceased, and Tonn took advantage of the brief lull to call out to his quartermaster, Matushenko, "Come down here and talk things over. We can still settle this without any more shooting."

Matushenko made his way aft and down the gang ladder as if impelled by automatic obedience to authority, escorted and covered by the guns of several of his closest henchmen. They were advising him against answering the summons to parley, but Matushenko shrugged their protestations aside. Still with his revolver drawn, Lieutenant Tonn disappeared through the main hatch into the 12-inch gun turret, and Matushenko followed.

If any words were exchanged between the two men, they must have been brief, for almost at once two shots rang out, and simultaneously one of the escort hovering outside the turret fell wounded to the deck. Tonn was the first to emerge, and whether he was already wounded and whether it was he or Matushenko who had fired first will never be known. He died at once under a hail of bullets, and Matushenko, who stepped through the hatch unharmed and as calmly as any professional assassin a moment later, ordered him over the side. "We haven't found the captain yet, you know," he told his men when this had been accomplished. "Has anyone seen the captain?"

"Where's the captain?" another voice shouted out. "We want the captain—he's the man we want. We want the captain . . ." The cries rose like some bizarre chorus after the intermission, and the hunt was at once resumed. They had also forgotten Chief Surgeon Smirnov in the excitement, and the man indirectly responsible for the uprising might have remained unmolested if he had not attempted suicide in his cabin. The exuberant and purposeless firing that had marked the opening minutes of the mutiny had by then died and the sound of the revolver shot drew a number of the men to the bolted cabin door. Details of the sequence of events that followed remain unclear. All that is known is that Chief Surgeon Smirnov, suffering from knife as well as gunshot wounds, was next seen being dragged across the quarter-deck by a group of sailors. They were still taunting him with abuse, and telling him to get his teeth into the high meat he had tried to make them eat, as he floated away, thrashing about feebly, and at last drifted out of sight astern on the current.

*   *   *   *

The mutiny on the *Potemkin* now drew rapidly to a close that was as violent, pitiful and bloody as its melo-dramatic opening. Since Matushenko's first cry of appeal to the firing squad, events had followed with the swift confusion of any sudden mass uprising, overlapping, uniting and splitting asunder like cells in violent muta-tion. But the two final acts stood out so clearly that every man aboard the battleship—even those who were not witnesses—was later to recall them in detachment from the main orgy.

The first was set off by words of warning impelled by panic that raced from stem to stern of the *Potemkin*. They broke into the party watching the spectacle of the Chief Surgeon disappearing astern, splitting it asunder as if a shell had fallen among them. "We're blowing up!" came the cry, elaborated seconds later by the news that a party of officers was down in the main magazine busy fusing the ship's complement of mines . . .

At once the tide of fear and self-preservation carried some towards the ship's boats, and the bolder in scrambling hue and cry down the gang ladders towards the bowels of the ship. But the crisis passed even more rapidly than the warning of its approach, and some of those descending to the magazine met others dragging up Junior Lieutenant Alexeev, the officer who had stood by Captain Golikov during his ineffectual harangue and had retired with him before the mutiny had begun.

"We found him trying to fuse the mines," a breathless sailor explained. "He was going to blow the lot of us sky high. We got him just in time."

"Let's have him over the side like the rest of them."

Matushenko met the party as they emerged on to the upper deck and ordered them to restrain their violence. "So there was only one of you, was there?" he demanded. "Who sent you down to the magazine?"

"The captain," Alexeev told him. "He told me it was better to sacrifice the ship than let you get control. But I'd like to join you. Don't kill me—I was always on your side, you know."

Alexeev had been the least unpopular of the officers, applying discipline leniently and occasionally showing almost comradely qualities. "All right, strip off his epaulettes and let him go," Matushenko ordered. "We'll see about him later. The man we want now is the captain. The first thing you can do is to tell us where he is," he told the lieutenant.

"You'll find him in his cabin—that's where I last saw him," Alexeev answered surprisingly. Golikov's cabin had been one of the first to be searched; later it was discovered that he and Alexeev had fled first to the unoccupied admiral's cabin at the start of the firing and had only later retreated to the captain's cabin.

The last killing was a desultory, almost weary affair, lacking all the impulsive anger and abandon of the earlier hunt through the ship. In the eyes of the men it was Giliarvosky who had been the *Potemkin's* tyrant, Golikov little more than a figurehead seldom seen by the men. It could not have been easy to induce the urge to murder the man who eventually emerged on to deck before a jostling group óf men. He was without hat or shoes or trousers, dressed only in his shirt and underclothes evidently in preparation for the swim that would follow the planned destruction of his ship. Divested of badges of rank and all dignity and courage, he was a pathetic sight.

With a sailor holding him roughly by each arm, the captain was hauled before Matushenko. "I know I'm really to blame for all this," Golikov told him. "It's all my fault. But I hope you'll forgive me and show some mercy. There has been enough killing."

Matushenko did not answer for a moment, as if considering the validity of his statement. Perhaps the captain was right; there seemed little point in putting to death this wretched looking creature.

"Personally I have nothing against you," Matushenko said at last. "But it depends on the crew." And he turned away as if to absolve himself from responsibility.

Among most of the men gathered in untidy, uncertain groups on the quarterdeck, on the upper deck above and on the top of the big gun turret, the passion had ebbed with satiation. But like a multitude of mountain river tributaries, the currents of feeling, opinion and resolution in the *Potemkin* were ever-varying, and their strength and rate of flow during the eleven days that followed were as sensitive to temper and events as water-level to rainfall. At that moment there were still some among the crew who felt that a mutiny was hardly decisive while the captain remained alive, and others who still bore him a special grudge. Among these was Ordinary Seaman Sirov, recently demoted for some misdemeanour, and it was his petty grudge that decided Golikov's fate.

"He said he'd string us up to the yard-arm, didn't he?" Sirov suddenly called out. "He was going to kill us, so let's finish him off." He pushed his way roughly forward, several of his cronies following behind, and took the captain from his unresisting guard. No one raised any objection, and there seemed to be a total indifference to his fate. A few followed the shoving escort party to the ship's rails; but it was a quiet, cold, passionless killing: a single shot from Sirov's revolver, a quick almost shamefaced tipping of the body over the side. That was all; and no one bothered even to watch the half-dressed corpse slipping astern on the current.

*   *   *   *

Knowledge of the mutiny came late to the officers and men of torpedo-boat N267, and counter-action was longer delayed by incredulity and indecision. A mere half hour had passed between the first shot and the death of the captain, and Lieutenant Klodt's order to flee the holocaust was countermanded when the extraordinary report that officers were diving overboard from the battleship reached him. To steam closer to the *Potemkin* might, so to speak, compromise his neutrality; to steam away would be callously disloyal, and might also cause belligerent action. To challenge the 12-inch guns of the battleship by closing or retreating appeared equally suicidal. Lieutenant Baron Klodt, therefore, remained at anchor, content to await the arrival of any surviving fellow officers, observing through his glass the spectacle of figures scampering across the *Potemkin's* decks and falling through the air, disappearing momentarily beneath the sea, and rising to the surface to be greeted by a fusillade of rifle shots that tore the water into a little white frenzy about their heads.

Junior Lieutenant Vakhtin was the first to be hauled on to the torpedo-boat's deck, severely wounded and exhausted. The few words he uttered only confirmed what all aboard the N267 could now see. The crew of the *Potemkin* had run amok, and wholesale slaughter was in full swing. An officer more confident of the loyalty of his crew and more determined and decisive than Lieutenant Klodt, might at this point have torpedoed the battleship at point-blank range before the mutineers had time to organise themselves. Instead, he awaited the arrival of the last survivors, and then ordered the anchor up and full steam ahead. The little boat gathered way rapidly, and her commander swung her round through 180 degrees to escape past the *Potemkin's* stern towards the open sea. Beside him in the small wheelhouse his navigating officer was busy calculating the time it would take to reach Sevastopol. At her maximum speed of 25 knots they should be there in about eight hours. Lacking the new wireless telegraphy equipment, it was urgently important that they should arrive as soon as possible to report the grave news of the *Potemkin's* mutiny to Vice-Admiral Krieger.

They had passed the stern of the battleship and were at a range of just over half a mile when the first shot rang out.

*   *   *   *

The threatened escape of the torpedo-boat brought control and leadership to the mutineers. On hearing the cry of warning Afanasy Matushenko awoke at last to his responsibilities. Until the moment when the captain's body had been thrown overboard no more had been demanded of him than that of any barricade ringleader urging his men to action. But with sudden and decisive victory, new qualities which never before had been tested, were called for. Soon all the complex organisation of a great battleship and her restless, uncertain crew would be in his hands. But for the present it was still only action that was demanded of him.

"Man the guns and put a shot across her bows," Matushenko ordered. "That'll soon stop her. They can't get away, the fools."

There was ammunition ready by the guns for target practice, and two men at one of the aft 47 mm. guns required only a minute to load their weapon and lay it on the fleeing torpedo-boat. The first shot fell well ahead of the N267, the second sent up a little fountain closer to her bows. Two more shots cracked out, the N267 steamed on, close to her maximum speed now, showing no indication of changing her course. The *Potemkin's* crew milling about the quarterdeck watched anxiously and shouted encouragement and abuse at the gunners. The torpedo-boat was a swift, nimble vessel, which could tuck herself in close to the shore and be out of sight of the *Potemkin's* gunlayers long before the heavy armament could be brought to bear. "Don't mess about," came the cries. "Put a couple into her."

At once there was a deeper, louder crack from the *Potemkin's* stern. One of the 3-inch guns had opened up. The first shot fell short, the second went clean through the torpedo-boat's funnel. This time the response was instant. Lieutenant Baron Klodt put over the N267's wheel and took her in a tight half circle back towards the *Potemkin.*

To Lieutenant Klodt either course must have appeared likely to lead to destruction, but at least the mutineers could feel no special personal malice against himself and his two juniors, although it might be different for the officers they had picked out of the sea, now huddled in the little wardroom below attempting to dry out their clothes.

As the torpedo-boat came alongside, a gang ladder to receive her was lowered from the *Potemkin*, and Matushenko stationed himself at the head of it. "Come aboard," he called down to Lieutenant Klodt, "and bring the officers with you. Your ship belongs to the people, the same as this battleship."

"Shall we line them up and shoot them like the others?" one of the sailors close to Matushenko demanded. All the armed mutineers were standing about close to the rails, and after the torpedo-boat's attempted escape there were some still in a threatening mood.

"No, there's been enough bloodshed," Matushenko ordered, so that all could hear. "Let them alone now. Just strip off their badges of rank and lock them all up below. Comrade Mikishkin, you put a dozen trustworthy men into the torpedo-boat and tell the crew they take their orders from us. The N267 is a unit of the Free Russian Navy now."

* * * *

By three o'clock in the afternoon, with the summer sun still high in the sky, the *Potemkin* mutiny was all over. Ahead there lay a multitude of dangers, decisions and problems without precedent. At Sevastopol there was a powerful fleet that must soon track down and attempt the capture or destruction of the battleship. The temper of the 700 men, in the vast majority of whom the urge to mutiny had been forcibly induced, must remain always uncertain and unreliable and would demand constant stimulation. The vessel herself, with the insatiable appetite of any battleship, would equally demand constant coal and fresh water in vast quantities; and her crew the food supplies of a large village. Confined to the Black Sea by the Turkish-held batteries of the Bosphorous, for the present the *Potemkin* would have to rely for supplies and succour on Russian ports; and their arrival at any of these must inevitably lead to conflict on a vastly more terrible scale than the brief violence of the mutiny.

Considered in their total, the problems facing Matushenko could send the mind reeling. But for that evening he was concerned only with clearing away evidence of the strife, weighing anchor and taking the battleship and her satellite from Tendra Bay and the scene of her crime. "Get parties together, will you, and wash down the decks," he told Mikishkin. "It's bad to have this blood lying everywhere. Then let me have a report on Vakulinchuk's condition, he looked in poor shape last time I saw him."

Matushenko looked down on the quarterdeck, now almost cleared of men for the first time since the uprising, and saw the ugly testimony to the killing he had set in train: the discarded tarpaulin lying crumpled where it had been thrown aside, the untidy pieces of equipment— several hats, a revolver and two rifles—the red stains from Vakulinchuk's wound where he had fallen, and nearby and close to the turret the pool left by Giliarovsky, the first of so many hundreds to die in the mutiny and its aftermath. The scene presented itself to Matushenko as "a terrible but a triumphant picture".

CHAPTER II

A City in Revolt

THE great city and port of Odessa lies in the centre of a wide bay on the north coast of the Black Sea and some seven hundred miles south-west from Moscow. In 1905 it was the fourth city of the Empire, with a population of close on half a million. Ships of all nations carried away each year from Odessa's harbour some twenty million pounds' worth of maize, barley and timber, sugar, meat, poultry and other products of the farmlands and forests of Bessarabia, the Ukraine and the rich Dnieper Valley, and the coarse dried fish and unsurpassed caviare from the fishing grounds between the mouths of the Dniester and Danube rivers.

The city was regarded as one of the most beautiful in the Empire, the centre more closely resembling a prosperous French cathedral city than a traditional Russian provincial town of dusty or muddy streets and wooden buildings. The main thoroughfares were broad and tree-lined, bordered by wide pavements, balconied private mansions and shops; and the aristocracy, the rich merchants, bankers and manufacturers and their families drove up and down them in carriages or droshkis, the proletariat in modern single-deck trams. On Sundays and summer evenings the best people strolled along the Nikolaevsky Boulevard high above the harbour with its magnificent views across the public gardens to the bay and the sea beyond. They lacked none of the culture, comforts and conveniences of Moscow and St Petersburg. From the tower of St Nicholas's church the city presented an orderly aspect of green-shrouded squares and gardens, wide streets, the spires, minarets, and cupolas of the university and cathedral, the town hall and city library, the museum of antiquities, and the vast stone colonnaded Courts of Justice.

The impression of Odessa from St Nicholas's was one of gracious and elegant prosperity, and on most days drifting smoke or heat haze obscured the docks and more distant industrial areas. This was no loss to the sight-seer, just as their existence was mainly disregarded by those who lived in the centre of the city, where the frontier lines were as clear-cut as the class divisions accepted on both sides. To the north and north-east were the low-lying docklands, the wharves and ware-houses and smoky railway sidings and the great Belino Fenderich shipyard; to the north and north-west the more recently built outlying factory fringe, the scruffy suburb of Peresyp, where shoddy wooden shacks lay huddled in their thousands about the Roestal Ironworks, the Imperial Russian Cotton and Jute works, and the smaller heavy and light engineering factories.

Throughout most of 1904 the Far East war had little affected the industrial, business, municipal and social lives of the city. Many of the citizens regarded it as another, if more ambitious, private enterprise or punitive expedition of the Romanovs, in accord with the common expansionist and imperialist practice of the western powers. Such campaigns had become commonplace over the past fifty years. General Kuropatkin would, in the course of time, sweep the insolent Japanese back into the sea. Nor was there anything reprehensible about land-grabbing or the defence of appropriated territory, so long as you were successful; if you failed, as the British had in the early years of the Boer War, you were merely made to look ridiculous, and international opinion was of little account.

During the first twelve months of the conflict, while

the Eastern armies yielded before the fanatically keen and skilfully led Japanese and surrendered the entire peninsula of Korea, the people of Odessa had benefited rather than suffered. The city lost a sprinkling of eligible young men who entrained on the trans-Siberian railway in splendid uniform and it became necessary to replace some of the conscripted male labour with women in the factories and dockyards. There was perhaps a certain measure of anxiety among the educated citizens during the closing months of 1904, but unemployment was at a negligible level and there was even a sense of affluence as government orders continued to be met. Winters are mild on the Black Sea, and as a funnel for such vast food-producing farmlands the people of Odessa experienced none of the privations suffered in St Petersburg and Moscow. The city appeared an unlikely place for a revolution to start.

* * * * *

The tide of underground insurrectionist activity had ebbed and flowed through the Russian empire for the previous half century, rising with the hardships and the demonstrations of incompetence and corruption during the Crimean and Turkish wars; and falling again with the more liberal policies of Alexander II and the emancipation of the serfs in 1861. By 1894, when Nicholas II succeeded his tyrannous and formidable father Alexander III to the throne, the empire had incorporated by force new and troublesome territories in Asia and Europe and had tightened its hold over the nominally independent states of the Caucasus, Finland and the Baltic provinces. Poland, after the bloody and unsuccessful revolution of 1863 was as restless as ever. The situation in the Far East, where a new and unwelcome Japanese imperialism was demonstrating its power against China in 1894–5, was ominous and threatening. Nicholas's father's reign of uncompromising autocracy had also coincided with Russia's long-delayed industrial revolution, and the new Tsar inherited not only a number of half-barbarous states in the empire, but a huge and growing class of factory workers, all underpaid, all working together in large numbers and in close proximity, living in overcrowded conditions, and highly susceptible to subversion.

The first ten years of the reign of Tsar Nicholas II had seen a tremendous growth in the scope and organisation of subversive activity, ranging from mild and intellectual liberal reform movements among the educated upper-crust, through Menshevism, Bolshevism and their numerous bickering offshoots, to nihilist terrorism of the kind that had led to the assassination of Nicholas's grandfather and to innumerable bomb and shooting incidents in almost every town and city in the empire. This gathering revolutionary momentum, which was to lead to anarchy in 1905 and the end of the Romanovs twelve years later, had its primary cause in the character of young Nicholas and his inner caucus of diehard reactionaries, men like Vyacheslav Plehve and Konstantin Pobedonostsev, who believed that the uneducated masses were unfit, and should remain unfit, for any sort of responsibility in their own welfare, government and future. The vast sprawling mass of the Russian empire, stretching over thousands of miles and embracing tribal territory and huge populations speaking foreign tongues, could be held together only by an oligarchy possessing the combination of unrestricted power, a father-figure mystique, and strong military, police and secret counter-revolutionary forces.

Foolish if well-intentioned, charming, weak, conditioned by his upbringing to the acceptance of the dignity and divine power of his throne, Tsar Nicholas II

was bewildered and deeply offended by the sudden out-
bursts of violence that broke out from Vladivostock to
Warsaw, from the Crimea to St Petersburg, early in
1905. The terrible news of Father Gapon's march on the
Winter Palace in January, and the subsequent shooting
down of some five hundred of his passive demonstrators,
was closely followed by tales of greater disasters than
ever in the Far East, and the loss of thousands of men
and whole arsenals of equipment. It was an especially
bitter winter, and with the sudden cessation of armament
orders due to the imminent bankruptcy of the government, hundreds of thousands were thrown out of work
and desperate shortages of food coincided with the worst
of the winter weather. On December 28, 1904, Port
Arthur, long besieged, the cornerstone of military power
in Manchuria and only major naval base the country
possessed in the East, fell to the Japanese under particularly humiliating circumstances. Worse was to
follow. The Japanese drove on invincibly by land, and
in May utterly annihilated a vast, ill-equipped and
heterogeneous armada of battleships, cruisers and torpedo-
boats sent out from the Baltic half round the world in a
last desperate gamble to stave off defeat. The disaster at
Tsu-Shima at last convinced the Russian government
that there was no advantage to be gained in continuing
their cripplingly expensive and ineffectual campaign.

The common people had long lost what spirit they
ever possessed for this unpleasant, unnecessary and
bloody little war. By Tsu-Shima, and long before the
Treaty of Portsmouth in August, 1905, the workers
everywhere were engrossed in their joint struggle for a
livelihood and their liberty. In almost every community
from small towns to the capital itself, revolutionary cells
existed, eager to organise strikes and marches, ready for
violence where the need for it existed and when weapons

were available, and supported in spirit by many western nations, especially the U.S.A.

* * * *

Odessa had remained almost unaffected by the strikes and unrest elsewhere following the Winter Palace massacre. Working conditions in the city were far from satisfactory and there was much poverty and distress among the poorer and unskilled working classes, but the revolutionary leaders lacked the advantage of utter despair and starvation which had taken a firm grip on the more northerly cities and industrial towns, where marches and open air meetings and well-organised strikes caused daily clashes with the police and subsequent bomb-throwing and shooting.

But during the first weeks of February the situation began rapidly to change. "The local branch of the Social Democrat party found their efforts to rouse the people at first unavailing, but the economic conditions soon provided a more favourable field for their agitation," wrote a student* at the University of Odessa, which possessed one of the most active and successful Social Democrat cells. "Though the workers still found some sort of existence possible, there was great uneasiness among them, and a growing apprehension of the complete closing of the factories. The employers were cutting the hours of labour shorter and shorter with a corresponding decrease in daily wages. Many of the factories which had barely maintained their footing were closed altogether."

On April 21 the first major strike broke out in the docks, where the Bundists and Social Democrats had concentrated their activities and found especially favourable

* The Revolt of the *Potemkin* by Constantine Feldmann, trans. by Constance Garnett (1908).

conditions. Men of the Russian Steam Navigation Company came out *en masse*, and were followed at once by workers of the Russian Transport Company and Danube Company. Naval personnel were sent in to take over, but could deal with only the more important and perishable cargoes. The well-organised bakers came out next in protest against inadequate wages, working conditions which included a seven-day week, and the regulation that obliged them to sleep in lodgings supplied by their employers on the premises. The tailors, shoemakers, printers and butchers followed them; and the police, now alarmed at the growing crisis and signs of unrest among the factory workers, successfully urged the employers to come to terms. The agitators were quick to take advantage of this rapid capitulation and intensified their efforts, pointing out to the workers the strength of their position if they acted together. They had their first industrial success in Peresyp on June 12, when the jute workers came out, and aroused the first violence on the same day when members of a delegates' meeting were arrested.

The pace of events now rapidly increased, with every new idle worker, every angry word, every act of defiance strengthening the agitators' position. Trains running in from the north were halted in the suburbs by gangs of workmen and their wives, the locomotives' fires doused and the rails torn up. A huge demonstration converged on the police station in which the delegates were held, demanding their release, and on the police's immediate capitulation, marched back again in triumph singing the Varshavianka. The ironworkers, cotton workers and railwaymen struck on June 25, and the 27th was agreed among the various revolutionary parties as a date for a general strike throughout the city.

Odessa's military governor and G.O.C. troops, General Kokhanov, had at his command a regiment of Cossacks, substantial forces of well-armed police, and troop reserves at Tiraspol, Belets, Vender and Ekaterinoslav amounting to three regiments and a brigade, on which he could draw in an emergency. Kokhanov began to show considerable alarm at the situation and the well-organised nature of the revolt, and as a first step pressed the employers to convene a meeting of factory inspectors to discuss pay, working conditions and the nine-hour day, one of the workers' strongest demands. But the position was even more critical and the necessity for action even more urgent than Kokhanov had believed. Hour by hour the situation was deteriorating from civil disobedience to open revolt. On Monday 26 June, more than five hundred workers assembled outside the Gena works and Hoehn's plough factory at Peresyp to organise a protest march through the city. Kokhanov had full knowledge of this demonstration and ordered armed police there in strength, reinforced by a sotnia—a hundred—of Cossacks. Before any speeches could be made, the police intervened and a mounted captain rode up and ordered the men to disperse at the third bugle blast, or suffer the consequences.

The men could see the police formed up ostentatiously behind him, also mounted and armed with revolvers and sabres, and farther up the street the Cossacks, in their crisp, white jackets and peaked caps, black breeches, and high, black boots. Defiance could lead only to bloodshed, and most of the men were already in retreat when a shot was heard from the window of a nearby building at the second bugle blast, and a Cossack officer fell wounded from his horse.

That single revolver shot fired by an unknown revolutionary broke up civil order and discipline in Odessa as suddenly and dramatically as Seaman Vakulinchuk's rifle shot across the quarterdeck marked the end of authority on the *Potemkin* twenty-four hours later. For the battleship there was to be a sort of glory as well as notoriety, and fame for her mutineers. For Odessa there lay ahead only a period of civil strife and terrorism that was to result in the destruction of a large part of the city and the death of thousands of its inhabitants. No other town or city in the Empire was to suffer such disaster and bloodshed in the whole series of revolutions in Russia in 1905.

Within seconds the Cossacks had moved forward at a fast trot to avenge the wounding of their commander, firing from their revolvers as they charged, and then drawing their sabres to beat at the scurrying workmen. That first charge, supported by the armed police, should have dispersed the demonstration within a few minutes, and with grievous loss of life among the unarmed workers. The uprising might yet have been brought to a terrorised standstill but for the bold action of the men's wives who had been lurking in the background and now urged them to grab stones, counter-attack and, in turn, avenge the deaths of their comrades already lying on the dusty road. The effect of these cries of mixed mockery and encouragement must have astonished even the women. "A hail of stones came flying at the Cossacks," an eyewitness reported later, "and the valiant soldiers of the Don faltered, turned and fled in different directions pursued by the workmen. The workmen were triumphant at their victory. Some of them pursued the Cossacks, others began building barricades; two tram-cars and some carts were turned over . . . All Peresyp had risen by now, and we called the crowd to a meeting. Thousands of workmen from all parts of the town streamed to it . . . It was the first time I had seen such a majestic and mighty scene of the solidarity and brotherhood of the workers."

Ordered civil life had ceased to exist on the afternoon of Monday, 26 June, and the following morning the situation had become so threatening that Kokhanov established military law, ordered out all-night patrols into the streets and guards to the most important municipal buildings, and had posted all over the city a warning notice of three lines: "Yesterday in a conflict between the troops and the people, two workmen were killed and three wounded. The Governor calls upon peaceful citizens for the avoidance of accidents to abstain from joining the crowds of workmen."

It was clear from this that the authorities had accepted the inevitability of more demonstrations, and, because these were prohibited, of more bloodshed. It was, however, of vital importance to prevent any mixing of the classes. Kokhanov perhaps felt able to deal with massed formations of workers and their wives with the police and Cossacks under his command; but if the liberal and intellectual elements among the educated classes were to become involved then there was a real risk of civil war throughout the Ukraine.

The first shots were heard at eleven in the morning, when troops fired on a group of workers calling out on strike men at the Municipal Water Supply. Intermittent shooting continued until early afternoon, when the movement began to take definite shape, and workers with their wives, and even their children, marched in scattered groups towards the city centre, formed into larger and larger tributaries and flowed at last from dozens of sources into Preobrazhensky Street, the main artery and Champs Elysées of Odessa.

Groups of mounted police and Cossacks ranged to and fro in an attempt to turn back the demonstrators, sometimes sending them fleeing up streets and alleys, sometimes meeting a hail of stones and sticks and themselves being forced to yield. In Uspenskaya and Meschanskaya streets brief conflicts took place when passengers were forced out of trams which were overturned to form barricades reinforced with cobbles torn up from the roads, and the volleys of rifle fire were met by shouts of defiance, stones and isolated revolver shots. By late afternoon the Alexandrovski Prospect, Richelieu and Preobrazhensky streets were choked with shouting, cheering crowds that continued to swarm in from the docks and factory fringe of the city, smashing shop windows when the fancy took them, clearing trams and buses, droshkis, carriages and carts before them by sheer momentum and weight of numbers.

There was no apparent purpose behind the march, and it had achieved nothing but a proof of solidarity. Then, as hesitant as the waters of an estuary at the turn of the tide, the massed marchers in their thousands sought for a purpose and destination, and found neither. As a demonstration of strength they had succeeded in a spectacular manner. But the enemy's forces were still intact, lurking on their fringes with their rifles and sabres, with immense resources and the authority of ultimate power behind them. The rioters could smash in the windows of the Crédit Lyonnais and a hundred other offices, shops and private mansions, but the City Hall, the Governor's residence and military head-quarters, the Courts of Justice and Military Barracks re-mained under guard and the strict control of the State.

By early evening the tide began to ebb, tens of thousands drifting back, pausing momentarily to cheer a street-corner orator, to lend aid to a wounded man, to smash a window with half-hearted passion, to flee briefly from the threat of a patrol, but always heading out towards their wooden homes in the suburbs. There was no sense of fulfilment nor triumph at achievement among them, only frustration and purposelessness and anger at the casualties they had suffered.

What more could they hope to do without weapons?
The next day there would be no work, no food, no
future. They were obsessed with despair, saw salvation
in revolution but lacked all means of bringing about an
overthrow of autocracy. "The cry for arms rose up on
all sides," wrote Feldmann of that evening, "and we felt
that unless the Social Democrats could satisfy it, the
masses would turn away from us, and the strike would
be over." It was a dilemma that was to face every revolutionary cell throughout the country in 1905, which
possessed everything it needed for revolution except
the vital, catalytic ingredient of weapons. The power of
authority was limitless: infantry, cavalry, artillery
regiments, Cossacks, all well-equipped and seemingly
loyal to the Tsar. Between them the insurrectionists
could number a few hundred revolvers, a few dozen
rifles. There were bombs, of course, but little could be
accomplished with bombs; just the occasional assassination. At ten o'clock that evening a young Jew exploded
a bomb on his person while being arrested in the Cathedral Square. The sound of the detonation was heard all
over the city, and the Jew, the constable and a Dr Spivak
who chanced to be passing by in a droshki, were blown
to pieces.

More than a dozen Cossacks and policemen had been
killed in the past twelve hours, at the cost of several
hundreds of casualties among the workers, but no real
progress in the revolution, no destruction of the civil
government, could be accomplished without guns.
Bombs and barricades were not enough.

At eight o'clock that evening a battleship had been
seen to steam into the bay, accompanied by a torpedo-
boat. Some of the more knowledgeable among the
dockers making their way home along the quay beneath
the Nikolaevsky Boulevard identified her as the *Kniaz
Potemkin Tavritchesky*, the most powerful unit in the

Russian Imperial Navy, a great ironclad armed with
12-inch and 6-inch guns, and named after Prince
Gregori Alexandrovitch Potemkin, Catherine the Great's
favourite, and ruthless, first minister. It must have seemed
to them that retribution for their day of violence and
destruction had arrived swiftly and in awful strength.
In the twilight, and at the distance of four miles at
which she had anchored, it was impossible to recognise
that at her masthead and stern post the battleship flew
the red flag in place of the cross of St Andrew.

CHAPTER III

The Tsar Declares War

SEVEN of the *Potemkin*'s officers had died in the half hour of violence on the battleship, and of the eleven survivors, several had been wounded, Lieutenant Vakhtin seriously. Even Father Parmen, the large, heavily-bearded and inoffensive priest had been roughly handled by some over-excited sailor and had had to go to the sick bay for treatment by Dr Golenko.

Golenko, Surgeon Smirnov's assistant, was a small, pale-faced, bald-headed man, a careful dresser and a sad individual who was regarded more as a figure of fun than with respect or fear by the crew. This "typical pampered nobleman", as Feldmann called him, had decided to throw in his lot with the mutineers because "I feel it my duty to look after the sick and wounded among you and the officers". The motives of three others who joined him were less clear. Lieutenant Alexeev had already claimed that he had "always been on their side"; and two of the engineer officers responded so readily to Matushenko's suggestion that they should remain to supervise the engine-room staff, that they either lacked the courage to refuse or were naturally disposed to sympathise with the mutineers. These men were Lieutenant Kovalenko, a good-humoured young man with an amiable face and a crop of thick fair hair, who had never been heard to speak a cross word; and Midshipman Kalujny, an undersized, weak youngster, for whom the episode had been altogether too much to endure. All the other surviving officers were locked away in a cabin under guard, with Lieutenant Klodt and his two

51

midshipmen, while the decks were washed down and order was brought back to the ship. Their future remained uncertain, but unless a more extreme clique gained control their lives at least seemed to be safe for the present.

For the crew of the *Potemkin*, now tasting the first fruits of the Marxist revolution, the régime of democracy opened when Matushenko recalled them to the quarter-deck and informed them in a long speech—the first of so many—that the one thing they had all to recognise was the importance of discipline. Matushenko was a curious blend of the romantic and the realist, and was at his finest as an orator. At that moment the majority of the men were in such a wrought-up and emotional state of mixed exaltation at their triumph and awe at the crime they had committed and the blood they had shed that they could have been led in a daze of enthusiasm clear across the plains to the Kremlin itself. Matushenko recognised that this was a time for realism, that the men had to be made to recognise the facts of their position.

So Matushenko told them, from the same capstan on which the ship's captain and commander had in turn harangued them an hour before, that the maintenance of organisation was the first requirement now that the hated officers had been overthrown and the ship belonged "to the people". The term "comrades" was used many times, and there were many references to the glorious revolution and the liberty of the people and the destruction of the oppressors. He had lived among these men long enough now to avoid venturing into the realms of higher Bolshevik philosophy. With them you could not oversimplify an issue, and Matushenko, a small, tense, gesturing figure on his tiny island in an ocean of faces, explained the dangers as well as the exciting future that could be theirs if they worked and fought together in harmony.

"All Russia is waiting to rise up and throw off the

chains of slavery. The great day is near. And it is on
this ship that the revolution has started. Soon the other
vessels of the Black Sea Fleet will join us, and then we
shall link up with our brothers on shore—the workers
in the factories and the men who slave in the land.
Already revolts are breaking out all over our country—
agrarian uprisings in Bessarabia and the Ukraine,
strikes in the factories at Odessa and Sevastopol.

"We have here the most powerful ship with the most
modern big guns in the navy. The *Potemkin* can fight
whole armies and defeat them. But we shall be helpless
if we do not work together. That is why there must be
discipline. There will never again be tyranny in the
Potemkin, but there must be some to give orders and some
to carry them out if we are to win. So we must have a
People's Committee . . ."

The power of the Committee must be absolute,
Matushenko went on to explain, for without power there
could be no proper control. This Committee would
maintain in an enlightened form the discipline that had
prevailed before the mutiny, could authorise the arrest
and punishment of any bluejacket who broke the established regulations in the navy. It would also be responsible for any action taken against the Tsarist régime, and
any subsequent negotiations with it and with all other
revolutionary organisations; and it would also be
responsible for the money in the ship's safe. The sittings
of the Committee, in accord with correct Marxist
practice, would be public, for the *Kniaz Potemkin
Tavritchesky* was now a People's Democracy.

The election of the Committee was carried out with
brisk efficiency. There were to be thirty members, and
these places were filled, after rapid and noisy nomination
and the raising of some hands, by the ringleaders in the
mutiny, who were also the officially-accredited Social-
Democrat representatives in the *Potemkin*. As Deputy

Chairman of the Committee under Matushenko were Mikishkin and Dymtchenko. Fyodor Mikishkin was a tall, thin, dreamy revolutionary, "more like a philosopher than a marine" as Feldmann described him, a fine orator who was concerned particularly with the religious and humanitarian aspects of revolution, although he was always prepared if necessary to commit violence, and "throughout the whole rising, both in the Committee and among the crew, he championed the boldest measures". Josef Dymtchenko, too, was an idealist, but he was a dreamer without the power of initiative, a tender-hearted, irresolute man who had had leadership thrust upon him and quickly became distracted in moments of crisis; a good-natured, sentimental peasant, broad-shouldered and muscular.

Matushenko's third Deputy would have been Seaman Vakulinchuk. But while the crew of the *Potemkin* were assembled on the quarterdeck for this first mass meeting, Gregori Vakulinchuk lay in the sick bay under the care of Dr Golenko, dying from gunshot wounds. He was unconscious for most of the time, but according to those present, he regained consciousness when the ship was under weigh, and opened his eyes briefly to see a group of his friends gathered about his bunk.

"How is it with the ship?" he asked in a whisper.

"We have avenged you, comrade," he was told. "We have killed the officers, and the ship is ours."

"Good, good," were Gregori Vakulinchuk's last words before he died, to become the most famous martyr of the 1905 revolution.

*   *   *   *

The *Potemkin*'s People's Committee gathered in the admiral's stateroom immediately after the dismissal of the mass meeting, and made themselves comfortable in the deep leather sofas and armchairs, helping themselves freely to the wine and cigars. They were all conscious of a sense of well-being and optimism, and there was a certain amount of light-hearted banter about their new-found comforts before Matushenko brought the meeting to order.

There was, he told them sternly, no time for fooling. They were outlaws of the state. The hand of every loyal soldier and sailor would be turned against them, and they must expect attack by land and by sea. They must be prepared for battle. They must obtain at once fuel for their ship and food for the crew. They must link up with revolutionary elements ashore, and go forward with them together in the common cause.

With these general principles settled, Matushenko got down to practical details: they had to decide on a destination, and they had to elect captain and officers. The choice of a port likely to meet their needs was limited to Nicolaiev, Sevastopol, Batum, and Odessa. There were other minor ports and fishing harbours, but none was likely to have sufficient food and coal for more than a day or two. Of the main ports, the first three were fleet bases, and until they had certain knowledge that the main mutiny was taking place, it was wiser to avoid trouble from other units and shore batteries. Clearly, Odessa was the best choice. Before they had left Sevastopol, the strikes and unrest at Odessa had been common talk, and the word had been spread to all revolutionary cells that a general strike was imminent. There would be strong Cossack and other military forces in the area, but at Odessa they could be confident of the support of the large working population. Clearly the city of Odessa was the most favourable city in the south of Russia at which to start the revolution. They would go there, and declare war on the régime.

The choice of officers to command the ship and handle

her in any engagement was more difficult, and a long argument ensued among the Committee members on this point. The difficulty was chiefly psychological. While the average, simple-minded, illiterate bluejacket was sufficiently dissatisfied with his lot to follow any uprising that was obviously going to be successful and lead to an improvement in his conditions, he was also a creature of routine, trained to respect his superiors. The idea of being led by men without badges of rank and in uniform similar to their own, men with whom they had been living for months and sometimes years on equal terms, would give them an uneasy feeling of insecurity. Life in any ship depends on tradition and the complex structure of rank, and Afanasy Matushenko was perceptive enough to recognise that if the *Potemkin* was to function as an organised and effective fighting unit, a privileged hierarchy would have to be retained; operating not of course by fear, for the battleship belonged to the people, but by a proper respect for authority. And if only for reasons of expediency, it seemed sensible for the bo'suns, corporals and petty officers to retain their rank, and for an officer to run the ship. An officer, in command, would after all act as a credential of respectability in any negotiations, and would curb unruliness among the wilder element of the crew. The men were more accustomed to obeying orders from an officer than from Marxist extremists from the lower decks.

The Committee therefore decided unanimously that Engineers Kovalenko and Kalujny would continue in charge of the engine room, and that Lieutenant Alexeev should be appointed captain, under the supervision of the Committee, with bo'sun Mursak as chief officer. Alexeev later claimed that this appointment had been thrust upon him under duress, that he had acted at gunpoint from the beginning, but as he had numerous opportunities to escape if he had wished, this seems unlikely.

He was, in any case, no more than a puppet commander, a symbol of authority, taking his orders from Matushenko and his deputies, and in moments of crisis was ignored altogether.

*   *   *   *

On the short voyage to Odessa the immediate benefits of the mutiny may have seemed slight to some of the sailors of the *Potemkin*. They were still in the same *équipages* and companies under the same petty officers as before, worked the same watches, were subject to the same discipline with the same punishments for any infringements. The routine and management of the battleship remained unchanged. For that night at least, their only food would be bread, biscuits, and of course maggot-ridden *bortsch* if they chose. And judged on his performance that afternoon, Matushenko could be a more formidable and intimidating commander than Captain Golikov.

But there does not appear to have been either despondency or fear for the future on the lower decks that evening. An extra daily ration of a quarter pint of vodka was issued to the men, and rather more singing and horseplay took place than usual. But considering the historic importance of what they had that day accomplished, the celebrations were mild.

At Odessa the first street lights were being turned on as the *Potemkin* approached from the east, the tamed torpedo-boat N267 following at her stern, and the crew of the battleship saw the city first as a faint glow in the twilight against the hills beyond. Tomorrow they would land. The men reacted to this prospect in several ways, the more ardent revolutionaries seeing it as a glorious assault, with death amid the crackle of gunfire, followed by a linking-up with comrades, and a great march

forward to the revolution. For men like Matushenko and
Mikishkin who had been working for so long as cell
leaders within the service, the arrival off Odessa in their
own battleship must have been a stirring moment, the
culmination of their ambitions. There could be no going
back now; they were committed to insurrection, with all
its formidable possibilities and uncertain outcome. But
in spite of Matushenko's harangue, there must have
been many more in the *Potemkin* that evening who saw
the immediate future as a golden opportunity for riot
and self-indulgence, with a wide open port available
for their pleasure, and no naval police nor gendarmerie to interfere. They had enjoyed the mutiny and
now they looked forward with excitement to more
fighting.

The number who in spirit had opposed the mutiny and
had been horrified at the turn of events with the overthrow of established authority will never be known.
But they were many, perhaps, a third of the ship's
complement of 700; and the pressure of their influence
would always be felt on board and would later decisively
affect the turn of events. Among them there could have
been only alarm at what lay ahead, at the proposed
landing and link-up with the strikers in the city and the
instigation of revolution throughout the Ukraine.

Feelings of fear, of triumph and fulfilment, of excited
anticipation, were all present in the *Potemkin* when
she dropped anchor in the wide bay just outside the
harbour entrance at ten o'clock on the evening of
June 27.

*   *   *   *

The young man who was to take a leading part in the
events that followed the mutiny on the *Potemkin* was by
chance one of the last to hear of the battleship's arrival

off Odessa. He was Constantine Feldmann, a student at the university and one of the leaders of the large Social-Democrat cell there. On the previous evening he had visited Peresyp disguised as a worker, and had been a witness to the despondency and frustration of the demonstrators on their return from the march to the centre of the city. "What had the morrow in store for us?" he wrote* later of that evening of critical uncertainty. "Everyone of us fell asleep that night with that question in his mind, and no one found the real answer."

The following morning, still in workman's clothes, Feldmann left his lodgings at ten o'clock for the house of a fellow student. He walked down through the main streets of the town towards the Nikolaevsky Boulevard and the great flight of the Richelieu Steps, which climbed from the harbour area to the boulevard and the statue of the Duc de Richelieu himself, the famous French émigré and governor of Odessa in 1803, who had been largely responsible for the growth and development in importance of the city. Feldmann was surprised to find the streets again full of strikers and curious crowds in spite of the ineffectual demonstrations and protest meetings of the previous day, and was conscious of a new excitement and sense of approaching crisis.

It was not until he arrived at his friend's flat that he heard the astonishing news that a battleship and torpedo-boat had sailed in the previous evening, and that at daylight it was seen that they were flying the red flag. Feldmann quickly changed into his student's clothes and ran down to the Nikolaevsky Boulevard where he could see in the distance across the bay the dark silhouette of the battleship.

"I stood in dumb, awestruck ecstasy before this marvellous apparition," Feldmann wrote. "But there

* Feldmann, *op cit.*

was no standing still for long—one must hurry down
to it; the work that had been begun must be finished,
the great battle must be fought at last . . . and with
the joyful feeling of a soldier, who at the very moment
of retreat suddenly sees powerful and unexpected
reinforcements approaching, I rushed down to the
port."*

A vast crowd had preceded Feldmann. He could see
them below in their thousands, filling all the wide
cobbled quayside and swarming in greatest density
about a grey rectangle placed on a harbour quay near
the base of the Richelieu Steps and apparently guarded
by four armed bluejackets with fixed bayonets.

It was a curious time and place to pitch a tent.

*   *   *   *

On the evening of June 28, C. S. Smith, the British
Consul-General in Odessa, telegraphed in cypher to the
Foreign Office: "Battleship *Potemkin* arrived last night.
Crew has mutinied on account of an officer having shot a
bluejacket and has killed all the officers except three,†
apparently sympathisers. The corpse of the sailor has
been landed. Insurrectionary speeches are being made
over it to crowds who are shouting Liberty! Authorities
dare not approach nor interfere because in that case it is
threatened to bombard the town. Ship is coaling and
provisioning, paying liberally for everything. It is alleged
that the rest of the fleet have also mutinied and are
coming."

Lloyds was at once acquainted with the state of
affairs, and shipping companies with vessels in the
Black Sea or about to pass through the Bosphorus were
warned of the danger.

* Feldmann, *op cit.*
† This was of course an exaggeration.

The *Potemkin's* People's Committee had sat through most of the night trying to agree on a programme for the following morning, June 28. The final decisions were:

1. To send representatives ashore to negotiate the purchase of provisions.

2. To acquire coal for the ship's bunkers.

3. To carry ashore the body of Gregori Vakulinchuk, to be placed in state, and carrying an inscription, where it could be seen by the working people of the city.

4. To issue a communiqué describing the events that had taken place at Tendra Bay the previous afternoon.

5. To address appeals to the people of Odessa, to the Cossack regiment, and to the French Consul.

6. To make contact with the Social-Democrat organisations ashore.

Orders were issued to the petty officers to arrange for these decisions to be carried out urgently, for much had to be accomplished this first day, and counter-measures could be expected now that news of the mutiny must have reached Vice-Admiral Krieger at Sevastopol.

Soon after dawn a boat was lowered and a party of sailors rowed into the harbour, heading for the docks. Provisions were not to be seized irregularly. The purchase was to be carried out in accordance with regulations, and the official requisition form was in the name of the Imperial Russian Navy, and of Tsar Nicholas himself. Payment presented no problem. The ship's safe was found to contain some 24,000 roubles, equal to about £2,400, and the necessary shopping money was carried in the boat.

An hour later Gregori Vakulinchuk's corpse was brought up from the sick bay in solemn silence, and lowered overboard into a cutter. The lid of the coffin had been removed, his hands crossed over his breast, and his face was set in the calm, resigned expression of the martyr. Secured to his jumper was a notice to the workers of Odessa:

"Before you lies the body of Gregori Vakulinchuk," it read, "a sailor savagely killed by the senior officer of the battleship 'Kniaz Potemkin' for complaining that the *bortsch* was bad. Let us make the sign of the cross and say, 'Peace to his ashes'. Let us avenge ourselves on our oppressors. Death to them! And hurrah for freedom!"

The guard of honour carried with them ashore arms to resist any interference from the police and the Cossacks, and a sailcloth and spars with which to erect a tent. They had orders to remain beside the body until a funeral could be arranged.

Another party left the ship soon after the funeral cutter to reconnoitre the docks and report back on the coal situation. Even at anchor the *Potemkin* consumed several tons of fuel a day, and at full speed (which would surely be demanded of her as soon as the fleet sailed from Sevastopol) her consumption rose to a very high figure. It was urgently important that her bunkers should be stored to capacity. At mid-day the reconnaissance party reported that there was a half-loaded collier, the *Esperance*, with 160 tons, tied up in the harbour, and the torpedo-boat was dispatched at once to tow her to the *Potemkin*.

* * * *

Those first hours of June 28 were filled with purposeful activity, and the spirit of most of the men was high. There would be shore leave and a night on the town that evening—or a battle. In the first flush of self-confidence and consciousness of their power, they looked forward to either with equal relish.

The sense of omnipotence these men felt was reflected in the manifestoes and ultimatums that were taken ashore by yet another party during that first morning. "We ask all Cossacks and soldiers to lay down their arms at once in surrender and unite with the workers of Odessa in the common cause," read the ultimatum addressed to the military. "Down with autocracy! We have already endured the last hour of our suffering, and now we shall free the people of Odessa and of all Russia. If resistance is offered to us, we beg all peaceful citizens to leave, for we shall bombard the city with our guns." It was, as the Russian government later conceded in an official bulletin, a formal declaration of war.

The bombardment of the city: that was the dominating topic of conversation among the strikers, the upper classes, the administration and the military in Odessa, and among all the crew of the *Potemkin*, from dawn on the morning of June 28. General Kokhanov had every cause for alarm. The power of the naval gun had increased enormously since the city had been the subject of a desultory shelling by a combined British and French naval force during the Crimea War. The *Potemkin's* four 12-inch guns in two turrets fore and aft were of the most modern type in the Imperial Navy, and their specification matched those of any other navy. Constructed at the state gun factory at Obukoff on the Neva, these 40-calibre weapons could hurl a high explosive shell of some 730 lb to a maximum range of 20,000 yards, although their accurate range was less than this. At a rate of fire of one shell every three minutes from each gun, the *Potemkin* could, therefore, have poured into Odessa some twenty-five tons of high explosive from her main armament, and almost as much again from her secondary armament of sixteen 6-inch and fourteen 3-inch guns, in the course of an hour's sustained shelling. In addition, she could out-range, out-gun and out-manoeuvre every other capital ship in the Black Sea Fleet.

The situation that faced the authorities was alarming in the extreme. By far the most formidable single weapon of destruction that Russia possessed was in the hands of a group of violent insurrectionists, who had already shown their determination first by killing or wounding most of their officers, and second by threatening to destroy by gunfire the fourth largest city in the Empire. This situation would have been delicate enough in ordinary circumstances; but at a time when the peasants* as well as the factory workers, miners, shipyard workers and every branch of industrial worker were poised on the brink of violent revolution, the circumstances were dangerous indeed. From St Petersburg *The Times*' correspondent cabled that in the capital "a revolution is not only admitted as a possibility, but the word is even being applied to the present occurrence. It may be said without exaggeration," he went on, "that the Odessa mutiny has made a far greater impression on the ruling classes than the defeats in Manchuria and the annihilation of the Baltic Fleet combined."

This naval disaster, this final blow to the hope of averting defeat in the Far East had synthesised a multitude of strains of despair throughout the armed forces as well as the civil population and had tipped the scales in favour of the revolutionary movement in thousands of factories and villages. The twenty-three warships that had gone down in the Battle of Tsu-Shima had taken with them some five thousand sailors; as a high proportion of these were subverts who had plotted mutiny time

* "From every source one hears of the peasantry being in open revolt all over this and the surrounding districts. Fire-raising is one of the principal weapons in use, and yesterday the residence of General Tschertkoff—the former Governor General of Warsaw—was in great danger. In every village without exception there are agents of the violent revolutionary party doing their utmost to stir the people up to attack 'proprietors'." Dispatch from the Consul-General in Odessa.

and again, perhaps it can be said that they had not all died in vain, for a month later, to the hour, Afanasy Matushenko had succeeded where they had so often failed; a battleship of the Imperial Navy was flying the Red Flag.

In St Petersburg Tsar Nicholas countered the *Potemkin's* ultimatum to his troops and the threat of destruction of the city by issuing a ukase which began, "In order to guarantee the public safety and to put an end to the disorders at Odessa and in the neighbouring localities, we have found it necessary to declare a state of war . . ."

CHAPTER IV

The Martyr on the Quay

"COMRADES, there are thousands of us here, and none of us will stand for the slavery and oppression of the government any longer. Sailors, workers, dockers, leave your ships and your benches and let's all march into the town together. With rifles, and under the protection of the *Potemkin's* guns, we can win our freedom." Seaman A. P. Brzhezovsky, one of the *Potemkin's* escort party who had changed his role from solemn bier-guard to rabble-rouser, leapt down from the crate with a final shout, urging on the crowds close-packed on the cobbles about him.

By the middle of the afternoon, the body on the quay was still the rallying point for strikers and spectators. All through the hot morning the people had gathered, some out of curiosity, many to do honour to the sailor who had died in the cause of freedom and to leave offerings for the cost of his funeral. Never in the history of martyrdom can homage have been so prompt. "It was impossible to move," Brzhezovsky told Matushenko later. "Everyone wanted to look at the dead man. Many people approached, took off their hats, crossed themselves and bowed down to the earth before the victim of savagery and tyranny. Women wept and kissed the hand of the dead warrior of the people. Sobs were heard, and there were tears in the eyes of many men."

But reverence and sorrow changed to anger and demands for reprisal as the hot day wore on. Barrels were procured by some of the more eager orators and their supporters and a platform set up on them, from which spokesmen for the city's various revolutionary organisations—the Bundists, the minority and majority cliques of the Social-Democratic party, the Mensheviks, Poale-Zionists and Anarchists—in turn delivered passionate speeches to the crowds. Party differences were for the moment forgotten, and in rapid order resolutions, decisions and calls for action were passed amid shouts and barrages of invective against the tyrants and oppressors they accused of starving and working them to death. Then at unpredictable moments, scattered parties, suddenly yielding to the appeals for action, filtered noisily away from the main crush, calling out slogans and waving hastily-constructed banners, and made off up the Richelieu Steps and against the tide of fresh demonstrators towards the centre of the city. Their intentions were as undefined as they had been for the mass demonstration the previous day, and but for a few pistols, they were still unarmed. But this time they knew there was a battleship behind them. They had the promise of support from the triumphant sailors of the *Potemkin*, and could even see her black hull and the barrels of her great guns across the still water of the harbour. They had an ally, whose strength was greater than all the forces of the gendarmerie, police, Cossacks and soldiers together. They marched into the town in disorderly groups with faith in the power of the *Potemkin* and new confidence in the revolution.

*   *   *   *

The mayor of Odessa had responded quickly to the news of the *Potemkin's* arrival in the harbour. He took the first morning train for Moscow and St Petersburg, leaving a message with the Council that he felt it his duty personally to acquaint the government of the critical situation in the city. From a railway station *en route* he sent a telegram to his citizens "beseeching them to keep calm and to cease taking part in disorders". His business in the capital unfortunately kept him occupied until the crisis was over; and both the civil and military responsibility during this difficult time therefore rested on the shoulders of General Kokhanov.

By mid-day on June 28, the general was becoming desperately anxious about the situation on the quay. He was faced with a dilemma unique for a G.O.C. established in the heart of a great city. Alone he was responsible for the lives of over 400,000 civilians, some three-quarters of whom were on strike, were active revolutionaries, or were sympathetic to the aims of one political party or another dedicated to overthrowing existing authority. For more than twenty-four hours life had stopped in Odessa, and trade, transport and every department of administration was at a standstill; although for the present the centres of government and power were secure.

The immediate danger, of course, was civil war. This could be staved off only by preventing riots, incendiarism and mass murder of the ruling classes. He also knew that every engagement between the police or the Cossacks and the demonstrators, every sabre thrust and shot, increased the danger of complete anarchy and massacre. It had taken the death of only one striker out at Peresyp to initiate the entire general strike.

The knife-edge precariousness of the path that Kokhanov had to negotiate has been faced a thousand times by military governors of disturbed cities. But the sudden intervention of the *Potemkin* increased the delicacy of the situation a hundred times. The imponderables were legion. When could Krieger be expected with the rest of the fleet? How strong was the control of the mutineers on the battleship? Would they attempt a landing or would they first ship arms to the strikers ashore? Above all, would they really stand by their threat to bombard the city? The consequences of this last possibility were too frightful to contemplate, not only for the destruction the shellfire would cause, but also for the tremendous fillip that even a few salvoes would give to the enthusiasm and determination of the workers. But at the same time Kokhanov knew that if the situation deteriorated further, the risk of a bombardment was one he would have to face. From the windows of his H.Q. he could see the crowds sweeping down Preobrazhensky Street, into Nikolaevsky Boulevard, and down the Richelieu Steps to the quay, in ever more frightening numbers. The arrival of the corpse and the setting up of the bier earlier in the day had already posed one acute problem, and Kokhanov must have wondered many times later during the uprising whether he could not have avoided disaster altogether by acting promptly then and arresting the party. But at nine in the morning the news of the battleship's arrival, and the threat of her guns, were frighteningly fresh and he was given no time to make decisions.

While the crowds on the quay three hundred feet below were concerned only with paying homage to the dead sailor, Kokhanov held back his Cossacks, although orders had already gone out ordering up reinforcements from Belets and Tiraspol, Vender and Ekaterinoslav, and further urgent messages had been telegraphed to Sevastopol appealing for the intervention of the fleet.

Then soon after mid-day the telegraphed ukase from the Tsar arrived. The declaration of a state of martial law meant little, for Kokhanov already possessed the widest powers and had used them; what was more important was that it underlined the anxiety of the government, gave Kokhanov a free hand to use any means he chose to suppress civil disorders and suggested that he must on no account—and certainly at the risk of his career—allow conditions to deteriorate further. It

must have been this prod from the Tsar that decided
Kokahnov to take action when, towards mid-day, he
heard that the agitators and orators, rather than
Vakulinchuk's corpse, had become the centre of attention
on the quay. Later, when the first of the mobs surged into
sight up the Richelieu Steps, he ordered out a sotnia of
Cossacks from the Cathedral Square, where they w⁻
bivouacked, to quell any further disorders.

The tragic and horrible event that followed has been
immortalised in the famous steps sequence in Eisen-
stein's film, "The Battleship Potemkin". The Cossacks,
trained to deal with civil violence and less inhibited
about attacking their fellow-countrymen than the police
or even the army, had been humiliated in Peresyp on
the Monday and held back in a state of frustration from
breaking up the demonstrations on Tuesday, when the
barricades were dealt with mainly by the police, and
gendarmerie. All through that morning, while strikers
and sympathisers in their thousands marched shouting
through the streets, they had awaited the call to action.
When it arrived, it is certain that they were tensed up
and in no mood for compromise. Half the sotnia were
ordered to the head of the Richelieu Steps, the rest to the
quay by another route to cut off the demonstrators from
below.

The Cossacks' arrival coincided with the departure
for the city of a great crowd of demonstrators, the
vanguard of which had reached the top of the steps when
fifty mounted Cossacks bore down from both sides of the
Richelieu monument set in the crescent centre above.
The charging Cossacks, with sabres already drawn,
presented a picture of terrifying power and ruthlessness.
This was the nightmare scene which every worker and
peasant in the land had learned to fear from childhood,
and never expected to survive the slashing whips, the
sabre cuts, the synchronised volleys of rifle fire, and

lastly the thunder of hooves beating any survivors to
death as they tore past. It was the very stuff of Tsarist
tyranny.

But this time the crowd did not at first turn and flee.
The men leading the march were heady with a spirit of
new confidence and defiance. The fleet was behind
them. Already the greatest battleship was on their side,
and others would follow, they had been told. Hundreds
of armed bluejackets. Massive 12-inch guns, batteries
of 6- and 3-inch guns, quick-firers and machine-guns.
How could they fail with support on this scale? In any
battle, the *Potemkin* would open fire, the sailors down on
the quay had assured them. And such was the faith in the
power and invincibility of the battleship, that many of
the strikers must have imagined that high-explosive
shells, miraculously aimed on moving targets four miles
away, would at the last second single out the charging
Cossacks and blow them to pieces before their eyes. To
add good measure, they hurled sticks and stones at the
horses, and several shots rang out as the gap closed to a
few yards.

Unaccustomed to defiance. the Cossacks momentarily
reined in their mounts, and at a single word of command
thrust forward again. A few were lightly wounded, all
were seized with a determination to crush this sudden
and unexpected violence. With sabres raised, they
resumed the charge with renewed vigour.

The Richelieu Steps are some twenty-five yards wide
and made up of twelve flights, each of twenty steps, 240
steps in all, each flight broken by a broader step some
twenty feet deep. Massive blocks of granite up each side
act as a boundary separating the steps from the steeply
sloping gardens below the Nikolaevski Boulevard. It was
curiously appropriate and symbolic that the most
famous steps in the Ukraine, linking the grandeur and
luxuries of the rich boulevard with the unkempt and

unprepossessing dockland below, should be the scene of the first head-on clash in Odessa's civil war. They exist today, and will probably never be destroyed, as sacred a site to the people of Soviet Russia as Runnymede or Yorktown to the British and Americans.

The massacre that followed the temporary rebuff to the Cossacks took place down the entire length of the steps, reaching its culmination at their base. The leading demonstrators were thrown back from the crescent into the bottleneck at the top, those who escaped the slashing sabres and horses' hooves forcing back the hundreds more, who were still unaware of the Cossacks' onslaught and continued to fight their way towards the top. There were seconds of agonising, jostling confusion when tide met tide amid desperate shouts of appeal and abuse. And then the first shots rang out.

At the head of the steps a party of Cossacks had dismounted, and formed up with rifles raised. At the command of an officer, they aimed the barrels and fired point-blank into the panic-stricken, fleeing crowd of men and women, drew back the bolts of their rifles, descended three steps, crouched on to one knee—all in perfect unison—and fired again.

The dead and wounded rolled down step by step, some by their posture gathering speed and tripping and carrying the living with them others sprawling limp and inert across the steps. The weight and momentum of descent increased as the line of Cossacks advanced, rolling up the great stair carpet of humanity; squatting, firing, striding down three more steps over limbs and torsoes, firing again; pausing to fix bayonets then pacing down step by step in their high black boots, thrusting the long blades into the phalanx.

The second party of Cossacks galloped along the quayside and caught the delayed recoil from the rear of the crowd at the base of the steps. The alarm was still fresh and uncertain when the clatter of hooves on the cobbles caused the crowd to turn. At once it was clear that this was no simple dispersal of a demonstration, this was a killing operation. Sabres were raised high, and came slashing down as contact was made with the first of the fleeing crowd. Men, women, a youth or two, fell to the cobbles, sometimes screaming. From above the volleys of gunshots confirmed the reality: this was a massacre. Forced back on two sides, the rear of the crowd fell back north along the quay towards the crush around the bier, while others were forced into the water, or jumped down the twenty feet to attempt escape by swimming.

The two parties of Cossacks, one mounted the other still in parade-ground formation, met at the base of the bloody, corpse-strewn steps, joined forces and advanced at an order to continue the slaughter along the quay towards the still solid mass about the tent, bayoneting, firing, slashing with the rhythmic efficiency of a mechanical harvester through corn. The sticks and brickbats and slogan banners were trampled underfoot, the barrels and planks of the orator's platform swept aside.

Only the unguarded bier was left intact, and beside it the big wooden bowl of offerings from the people, a heaped pile of coins to pay for a martyr's funeral. Beneath the sail-cloth tent the corpse lay in its fresh linen within its coffin, in dignified contrast to the sprawled bodies in their private stains scattered about it on all sides, and in an obscene wide trail up the Richelieu Steps to the Nikolaevsky Boulevard above.

*   *   *   *

Leading members of the Social-Democrat party, which was by far the largest of the political groups in Odessa, recognised early in the day that they would have to

establish close liaison with the crew of the battleship.
Among them was Constantine Feldmann. However
excited he may have been at the first news of the arrival
of the *Potemkin*, Feldmann was a practical-minded realist,
and he paused only briefly among the crowd on the
quay to view Vakulinchuk's corpse, before procuring a
boat and persuading some workers to row him out.

The harbour was full of small fishing luggers and
rowing boats, all attempting to approach the *Potemkin*,
some carrying active revolutionaries like Feldmann,
others only idle sightseers. It soon became evident that
the crew of the battleship, who were anxious to prevent
confusion and a mass landing, were having difficulty in
holding them back. From all sides across the water came
cries of mixed greeting and congratulation, followed by
protests at being rebuffed. One naval cutter altered
course towards Feldmann's boat, and a voice called out
from it, "Where are you going?"

"To the free revolutionist ship," he told the small,
dark sailor at the stern.

"And who are you—a Social Democrat?"

Feldmann confirmed that he was, and was asked to
show proof. "I haven't got proof," he answered. "They
send us to rot in prison or Siberia without proof."

"All right, then, get in here with us."

Feldmann soon discovered that he had been intercepted by the leader of the mutiny himself, "our chief
and commander" as one of the sailors described him,
and on the brief journey to the battleship, he tried to
discover from Matushenko what were the immediate
plans and policy of the mutineers.

For Feldmann, the excitement that he had felt at the
sudden discovery that the fleet's most powerful battleship had mutinied and joined the revolutionary cause,
changed to sharp disappointment and dismay as soon as
he set foot on the *Potemkin's* decks. It did not take long to

discover that the great mass of the battleship's crew, while delighted at the new democratic régime which they had helped to create, if only by abstaining from opposing it, had no appreciation of the importance of the occasion. Rather than as a first triumphant round in a revolt that would soon spread to all the Ukraine and then to every corner of the Russian empire, these politically un-educated sailors seemed to view their mutiny as a bit of a lark and a good excuse for a beat-up ashore, as soon as they could get leave, or as a private settlement of old grievances, a purely parochial affair without heroics. The disillusioning fact that Feldmann had to face was that the *Potemkin* was no insurrectionist hotbed, eager for the overthrow of the tyrannous régime.

Already a note of caution could be recognised in the attitude of many of the Committee members, who had succeeded in persuading their leaders to follow a policy of restraint, perhaps in reaction to the uncontrolled violence of the previous afternoon. Any sort of landing and joint action with the strikers ashore was out of the question for the present. They would not contemplate splitting their forces and leaving the ship half-manned until reinforcements arrived. There would be no armed invasion, no support for the workers until the great mutiny succeeded. For the present the crew of the *Potemkin* were sitting tight within the security of their 14-inch steel armour plate; even Matushenko, it seemed, had either been tamed or had suddenly lost his resolve to join hands in a crusade against tyranny, until the fleet arrived from Sevastopol. "Their one firm and definite determination was . . . not to leave the ship under any circumstances, and not to take any decisive action before the arrival of the whole squadron," Feldmann wrote later. "From the Social-Democrat organisation they desired nothing but moral support."

If Kokhanov and the civil authorities ashore discovered

the real attitude of the *Potemkin's* crew, Feldmann realised, all prospects of success in the planned revolt
would be shattered, the general strike would be broken,
and the greatest chance they were ever likely to have of
overthrowing the Tsarist tyranny would be lost. At once
he and two other agitators who had arrived with him in
the admiral's stateroom, set about the Committee with a
rapid course of indoctrination.

The three civilians were all experienced orators, and
the effect of their impassioned speeches of appeal for
co-operation was beginning to show, they thought, when
the collier was towed alongside and the important
operation of coaling commenced. They may have heard
that in the navy everything stopped for coaling, but they
could hardly have anticipated such a violent interrup-
tion, nor such a sudden departure of most of their
audience. The roar of winches, the hiss of steam, the
shouts of the men and the crash of coal into the bunkers
made it impossible to continue, cut off all other sound
and, as Feldmann recorded in evident exasperation,
"we were condemned to a brief inactivity."

The three Social-Democrats remained below decks,
impatiently awaiting the completion of this vital piece of
naval routine. But even if they had come up from the
Admiral's stateroom, they would have seen nothing of
the events taking place ashore; for just as the cacophony
of coaling cut off all other sound, so the black cloud of
dust that rose above the battleship obliterated the city
and the quayside and the massacre taking place on the
Richelieu Steps.

*   *   *   *

A small celebration had taken place on the *Potemkin* to
mark the arrival of the collier, under tow by the N267,
with her precious load of coal. The crew of the *Esperance*,

and some dockers who had joined them, began to sing the *Varshavianka* as they drew alongside the battleship, and were answered by cheers from sailors in the *Potemkin*. To Matushenko and other veteran revolutionaries the scene was a simple representation of the solidarity of the workers, an occasion to which they had been looking forward for so long.

The first news that hundreds of workers and their women had been killed and that the sailors had been driven from Vakulinchuk's bier, leaving it unguarded, arrived only later in the afternoon when a boat drew alongside with an official deputation from the Social-Democrat Party appealing for counter-action and bombardment.

The *Potemkin's* People's Committee was at once convened again to consider the situation, and Feldmann and the two other unofficial representatives were allowed to be present and to take part in the discussions.

A more urgent appeal was now made for an armed party to go ashore to engage the Cossacks and take over the administrative buildings of the city before the situation became out of hand and further massacres took place. Again the Committee was adamant in its refusal. An armed party, to have any chance against a regiment of Cossacks, would have to be so large that it would leave the ship open to counter-attack. The crew must remain united, they argued; it was essential that there should be no dividing of their forces before the arrival of the fleet.

But what about your guns? countered the civilians. The workers are relying on your guns. They are their only hope against the forces of oppression. Ashore we are being slaughtered, one representative pointed out plaintively, while here you have great guns that could destroy the whole terrorist régime within minutes. A bombardment? Now that was something different, the Committee members conceded. Of course they could open fire, there was no difficulty in that. But what would they shoot at? They had no idea where the military H.Q. was, the army, police and Cossack units were scattered about the city, they did not have even a map of the city on which the Governor General's head-quarters, the City Hall or any other useful targets might be located. No, a bombardment also was out of the question for the present until the fleet arrived. In any case, it had earlier been decided to arrange a solemn funeral for Vakulinchuk, the huge procession for which would serve as a demonstration of the unity of the sailors and the workers. The Committee were confident that this, with the ever-present threat of bombardment and the mutiny of the military following the appeals already dispatched from the *Potemkin*, would lead to the capitula-tion of the authorities. No, there would not at present be a bombardment, or an armed landing. There was no call for hasty action, the deputation was told before being hustled away again. But steps would be taken to ensure that there would be no further outbreaks of violence. The people must be protected, the solidarity of the workers must be maintained.

Soon after the departure of the disappointed deputa-tion and while coaling continued on the battleship, a cutter left for the shore with four sailors. They carried with them a manifesto drawn up by the Committee and addressed to the French Consul, the representative of the one country which had known oppression and triumphed over it in revolution.

"Most honoured public of the city of Odessa," it read. "Members of the crew of the battleship *Potemkin* today brought ashore the body of a sailor, in the care of a guard, for ceremonial burial. Some time later, a boat arrived at the ship manned by workers, and with the information that the guard set up over the body was driven away by Cossacks.

"The crew of the *Potemkin* begs the public of Odessa:

1. Not to offer any hindrance to the burial of the sailor.
2. To help ensure that the burial takes place with all ceremony.
3. To persuade the police and Cossacks not to interfere.
4. To assist the crew of the *Potemkin* in obtaining provisions and coal.

"In the event of non-compliance with all the above requests, the crew of the *Potemkin* will be obliged to bombard the city with all their guns. We therefore warn the public, that in case of firing, all who do not wish to take an active part in the revolution, should leave the city at once. We would add that we are expecting reinforcements from Sevastopol shortly, when the situation will become even more critical."

It was perhaps as well for the cause of solidarity that this manifesto was not made public, for its mild protest that the naval guard over the corpse had been driven away might have given offence to the relatives of the hundreds who had died while paying homage to the martyr. To ask the people of Odessa to "persuade" the Cossacks not to interfere with Vakulinchuk's funeral arrangements also seemed a stiff assignment in the middle of a general strike, especially without the support of the *Potemkin's* guns.

On the evening of that first day, men like Feldmann and the other Social-Democrats allowed to remain in the battleship were beginning to wonder which side Matushenko and his mutineers were on. Clearly a strong propaganda campaign was urgently needed, and Feldmann planned a series of speeches to be given to the sailors during the evening and the following day. To support him he had a member of the Bund, and a fellow

Social-Democrat, Kirill, a tall, powerful peasant with a bushy blond beard and "a mighty voice"; an honest simple-minded man who saw the revolution in plain black and white terms, of the wrongfulness of terrorism and the justice of the equality of man. The young intellectual Feldmann could not have had a more suitable ally, although Kirill was already exhausted before he came aboard from the demonstrations ashore, and after making one fiery speech, stretched himself out on a chair in the Admiral's stateroom and fell asleep.

* * * *

Their failure to intervene in the massacre on the Richelieu Steps had in no way reduced the confidence of the strikers in the power of the battleship and her mutinous sailors, and all through the late afternoon and early evening a bombardment was hourly expected. The *Potemkin's* 12-inch guns remained a talisman; against them the forces of oppression would crumble, and the hated, murderous Cossacks would be blown to pieces by their high-explosive shells.

The *Potemkin* remained also a subject of great curiosity, and as soon as the coaling was completed, boats arrived alongside in such numbers that they could no longer be kept away. Some carried family parties of sightseers, who wandered all over the ship, down to the engine rooms, through the galleys and mess decks, even into the gun turrets, touching the machinery, asking innumerable questions, and getting in everyone's way. The decks were being washed down after the coaling, and they trampled the coal dust and tripped over the hoses. From time to time the exasperated sailors retaliated with squirts that were not entirely playful.

Others came with more serious intentions, and the speeches that were made by numerous amateur orators all over the ship drew groups of curious sailors, added to the disorder and brought a touch of unreality to the bank holiday atmosphere that prevailed on the decks.

After a time the sailors tired of this noisy and disrupting crowd, of the untidy landlubbers interfering with the traditional routine of the ship, of the men and boys who turned the ranging wheels of the quick-firers, the women who commented loudly on the cooking arrangements in the galleys, of the fiery young Social-Democrat girl who had attracted a large audience and informed the sailors that it was their duty to make a landing and rout the forces of tyranny. There was, after all, a limit to hospitality, even on such a day as this. The ship was their home, and mutiny or no mutiny, the decks of a naval vessel were sacred, and routine and cleanliness were a vital indoctrinated part of their daily life. They were, in short, thoroughly offended by these light-hearted capers.

Once expressed, the sense of indignation spread rapidly throughout the ship, and in a short time the cry of "Clear out the landlubbers!" arose. Parties of bluejackets scoured the lower decks and drove up indignant families, and well-intentioned orators were forced to break off their speeches and join the crowds being hustled down the ladders to their boats. The disembarkation was less violent than that of the officers on the previous day, but equally noisy and almost as rapid. By late afternoon the decks were clear of all unwanted strangers, the ladders had been drawn up, the watches were getting ready to change, and peace prevailed. On the mess decks, the satisfied sailors settled down to their domestic routine, to supper, at which they ate gruel and butter, and drank tea; and doubtless grumbled loudly at the ignorance and lack of respect of all civilians. Such incidents served to cement the loyalty of seamen to their profession, and to one another.

From across the water came the sudden sad rattle of a machine-gun burst. Evidently they were having more trouble ashore.

* * * *

But the long day for the sailors of the *Potemkin* was not yet over. All through that evening boats manned by persistent or anxious agitators and keen sightseers approached the battleship, to be sent back to the quay by alert lookouts. One small rowing boat, however, would not be deterred, and in spite of the threats of the sailors came hard alongside the battleship's hull.

"What do you want? You clear out—no one else is coming aboard," the men at the oars were told.

"But we've come about your appeal," was the plaintive reply. "We are delegates from our regiment."

Feldmann, who had been attracted by this exchange, leant over the rails and recognised the occupants as soldiers in uniform. "Let a ladder down to them," he ordered. "They at least must come aboard."

The thoroughly frightened soldiers, who must already have taken great risks in breaking out of camp, and would have been shot if found fraternising with mutinous sailors, hauled themselves up the ladder, and were soon standing, panting from their exertions, on the quarter-deck. "Brothers," one of them said at last, "the soldiers of our two regiments—the Ismailovsky and Dunaisky— have sent us to tell you that we are with you. You're quite safe if you go ashore, none of us will shoot at you. And as soon as you land, we'll come over to your side."

"And a good thing, too," a sailor replied, "or friends would be fighting one another. It's high time this happened. But we're not coming ashore yet, all the same. We're waiting for the rest of the squadron."

The soldiers left again within a few minutes, their

mission accomplished; and they could claim that, unlike so many others before them, they had not actually been forcibly hustled off the decks of the battleship.

Dusk was beginning to fall, and the rifle shots and bursts of machine-gun fire from the city were becoming more frequent.

*   *   *   *

The culminating excitement of that first day occurred shortly after the departure of the military delegation, when a sudden cry of alarm from a look-out spread the dreaded words "The Squadron!" throughout the ship. Within minutes the entire complement of the battleship was on deck, packed shoulder to shoulder against the rails and peering anxiously out across Odessa's wide bay.

Was this the beginning of the end, or the end of the beginning? Was this really the Black Sea Fleet at last? And if so, was it still loyal to the Tsar, or had the planned mutiny taken place, the officers overthrown or killed? There was no means of telling until the ships came closer, until the flags at the mastheads could be identified, or perhaps until the first shots rang out.

All that could be seen at first was a single column of smoke on the eastern horizon, then a small hull shape. Clearly it was not a battleship. "It's only the *Viekha*," a sharp-eyed sailor suddenly cried out. And soon they could all recognise the little 150-ton fleet auxiliary, a paddle-steamer used for transport, delivery and surveying. There was nothing to fear from her; she did not carry even a single 3-pounder gun. She had left Sevastopol two days before, calling at Nicolaiev *en route*.

On the *Potemkin* the flag of St Andrew had been run up in place of the red flag when the *Viekha* neared, and the little auxiliary saluted the senior vessel and asked for instructions. Matushenko ordered the standard reply to be made, and sent a signal instructing the *Viekha* to anchor to starboard of the battleship and her captain to come aboard to report.

* * * *

The late Captain Golikov's wife, standing with her baby in her arms on the *Viekha's* deck, had expected to see her husband on the *Potemkin's* bridge, and was ready to answer his greeting. But there was no sign of him, and she presumed that he was either in his cabin or had gone ashore on some business. She watched the *Viekha's* commander in full dress uniform descend to a boat and be rowed across the narrow strip of water separating the two vessels, and climb out onto the companion ladder to pay his respects to his senior officer. There was no sign of the *Potemkin's* captain or of any other officer standing ready to greet him on the quarterdeck, and this was unusual. It was strange, too, that there were so many sailors on deck at this time of the evening, many of them carrying rifles, and congregated in a loose crowd instead of in ranks about the head of the ladder.

Madame Golikov's mild surprise changed to sudden anxiety when she saw the bluejackets close in round the captain the moment he set foot on deck, thrusting their rifles at him, waving their arms and apparently shouting threateningly. In the centre of the mêlée there was a dark sailor, shorter than the others, confronting the officer with a revolver.

* * * *

"You're under arrest," Matushenko told the *Viekha's* captain sharply. "This ship belongs to the people now. Hand over your sword and epaulettes."

The officer backed away in astonishment, to find himself hemmed in on all sides. "There's no reason to do me any harm—I've always treated my men fairly," he said.

"All right, we'll talk about that later. But hand over your sword and epaulettes quickly, and the sentry will look after you."

"You must let me return to my ship," continued the officer. "I shan't try to escape, but I have responsibilities there——"

"What sort of responsibilities?" a voice demanded.

"I have a woman with a baby on board."

"Your wife?" another sailor asked in mock disbelief.

"No, someone else's."

This was met by a chorus of laughter.

"I must go and protect her," the officer persisted; and the laughter changed to angry cries, while Matushenko raised his revolver threateningly and demanded, "D'you think we're criminals or something? We won't touch her. Now go below before you get hurt."

The rest of the *Viekha's* officers were next summoned on board, similarly deprived of their arms and epaulettes, and sent under guard to the admiral's stateroom, where they joined their captain and some hundred spectators from the *Potemkin's* crew. There, too, they were treated to a rousing speech by Feldmann, who acted to perfection the part of chief fire-eating propagandist to the revolutionary cause. "At last the day has arrived," he concluded, ostentatiously swinging his revolver to and fro, "when the long-suffering, downtrodden people of this country are rising up to cast judgment on their oppressors for their crimes."

Feldmann claimed later that his speech made a powerful impression on the captive officers, and that they had turned green with fear; but in fact their period of anxiety was brief, for the sailors of the *Viekha* had already despatched an urgent plea to the *Potemkin's* People's Committee begging them to spare the lives of their officers who had always treated them fairly. Evidently the *Viekha* was a happy ship.

So there was to be no more bloodshed on the battleship that day, and the captain and officers of the *Viekha* together with Madame Golikov and her baby, were at once put ashore, each officer, in a sudden gesture of magnanimity, being presented with one hundred roubles. That night the bereaved lady was taken to see the body of her husband, lying with others taken from the sea the previous day by the N267 and landed earlier.

*   *   *   *

For the men of the *Potemkin* it had been a packed and memorable day, and one which they could look back on with satisfaction. They had, after all, succeeded in revictualling their ship and adding substantially to their supplies of fuel; they had taken hero Vakulinchuk ashore and presented the people of Odessa with a martyr; they had succeeded in making their influence felt with the authorities, and yet had suffered no casualties and wasted none of their precious ammunition; they had acquired another vessel (and 2,000 roubles, less the officers' gratuities) and could justly call themselves now a rebel squadron. The *Potemkin's* decks were cleared for action, and they were ready to meet friend or foe on the morrow.

As night settled over the bay, the sound of sporadic gunfire increased in intensity, and from the warehouse area down by the docks the flames of a fire sprang up. There was still trouble ashore. But of course they were helpless to intervene. As the People's Committee had informed the workers' delegation that afternoon, it would be most unwise to split their forces at this stage: "United we stand, divided we fall." If only those demonstrators would restrain themselves until the rest of the fleet mutinied and joined them.

Meanwhile there was conflict, on a more restrained note, on the battleship. Since the ejection of the last civilians, a body of opinion had grown which sought to rid the ship of the leading Social-Democrat agent and his two companions. They were a thoroughly disturbing influence. Ever since he had come aboard nearly twelve hours earlier, Feldmann in particular had been roaming the ship gathering groups of sailors around him like some tub-thumper in a village market square, at first attempting to stir them into an armed landing, and when this lost him his audiences, proclaiming in emotional terms their responsibilities in the revolution that lay ahead. The man was nothing less than a fanatic.

Feldmann was fully aware of this antagonism, and determined to still it. His great chance came that night, with a captive audience of seven hundred, when the People's Committee convened a meeting of the ship's entire company. It took place in the hot and foetid atmosphere of the gun deck, in uncomfortable proximity to the main galley and engine rooms, with the sailors formed in a great semi-circle, the front rows sitting, the rear rows standing, and with Lieutenant Alexeev, Matushenko, Dymtchenko, Feldmann and the Bundist in the centre.

A formal summary by the ship's puppet captain on progress to date and an engineer's report was followed by a brief speech by Dymtchenko to introduce the representatives of the Social-Democrat party—"good men who want to say a word to us". At once the cry went up, "Put 'em ashore!" "Get rid of the landlubbers!" Didn't they have enough troubles on their hands already? This outside interference was intolerable. Almost the whole crew joined in the chorus of protest, making it impossible for Feldmann to begin to speak. Dymtchenko glanced across at him, hands raised, his face expressing helpless despair.

But after a while the cries of protest fell sufficiently for Feldmann to get an unwilling hearing. The young student must have been a brilliant orator, for in a short time there was silence on the gun deck, and he held the sailors for some two hours while he described the coming revolution, the evils of the Tsarist régime, the sufferings of the working people. He gave them a graphic account of the march on the Winter Palace and the massacre that followed. "The workers of Odessa have already shown proof of their loyalty to you," Feldmann told them, "and you are the first who have dared to build a bridge between the Tsar's forces of oppression and the workers and peasants who are struggling for their freedom. Let us march boldly over that bridge and link up with the masses in the coming revolution."

The sailors were spellbound, they had never heard anything so stirring. This added point and justification to their mutiny. It was not just the maggot-ridden *bortsch* and the grudge they bore their officers which had caused them to fight tyranny with violence. They were the vanguard of a great national uprising that would sweep injustice and cruelty from the face of all Russia. This was tremendous news. They were already heroes. A great burst of cheering greeted the end of Feldmann's speech, and there were cries from the audience for more.

Only the orators seemed conscious of the unbearable heat and stuffiness of the gun deck. But yes, there would be more speeches, willingly given, if first the men would move to the quarter deck, out into the open where they could all breathe. The men followed their leaders with enthusiasm, their appetites for oratory seemingly insatiable. Fortunately Kirill had by now woken up to lend his support to the team, and he climbed up on to the capstan to continue where Feldmann had left off.

It was chilly on deck in contrast to the stuffy heat of packed bodies below, when the tall uncompromising figure of Kirill climbed up on to the capstan and began appealing to the men for courage. "His voice rang out musically in the darkness of the night," Feldmann described this moment, "and it seemed that it was a ray of light penetrating just such darkness enfolding those downtrodden men till that day."

*　　*　　*　　*

All that night the words flowed unceasingly on the *Potemkin* as if the delayed shock of the mutiny had brought the men's excitement close to hysteria. When the mass meeting was broken up by the call to members of the People's Committee to convene in the admiral's stateroom, the crew formed up into smaller groups all over the vessel to continue talking. While plans were made at an official level below, conversation and argument went on unceasingly, on the quarterdeck, gun deck and main deck, on the forecastle and bridge, and below on the mess decks and in the living quarters. No one thought of slinging their hammocks that night. There was too much to talk about—from reminiscences of the violence of the day before, of the officers they had killed and others they had spared, to arguments about the speeches they had listened to and speculation about the likely outcome of their meeting with the main fleet. In the early hours of the morning the men were still talking and the Committee was still in session. Both Feldmann and Kirill had sore throats.

The searchlights swung their yellow fingers ceaselessly about the battleship, rhythmically up and down, round and round, searching the black water for landing parties or perhaps a venturesome loyalist torpedo-boat. Their criss-crossing pattern made a pretty sight. Odessa, too, presented a spectacular scene. Vast fires were blazing all over the dock and warehouse areas, and sudden gouts of flames lit up the undersides of rolling black smoke clouds. From time to time parties of sailors broke off their conversation to stand by the rails and watch the sight of half a city in flames and to listen to the sound of distant guns. Many would have liked to go to the aid of the workers, but knew that they were unable to help until the squadron arrived and they could risk dividing their forces.

The Committee members came up later to view the sight, and were affected by a similar feeling of impotence. The sound of shooting was growing in volume, the bursts of machine-gun fire were more sustained. But Lieutenant Alexeev tried to make light of it. He was sure the crackling came from burning timber and from roofs falling in. This "reassured us somewhat," recorded Feldmann, who was unhappy about the state of affairs ashore.

CHAPTER V

The Burial

N O one will ever know how many died in Odessa in the bloodiest night of the 1905 revolution, but most estimates put the figure at around six thousand. The dead were never counted. Nor will it ever be known just how and where and at what time civil strife grew into massacre, incendiarism and anarchy. As in any riot on this scale, there was no one who could describe afterwards the events in any detail, nor even their scale and sequence. Flight and fear and sudden moments of panic obscured all record and coherent memory of that bloody night as effectively and as finally as the sweeping flames and falling buildings obliterated human lives. Only scattered pictures, like a handful of stills from some epic horror film, were left to those who survived.

Certainly the first reports were wildly inaccurate and over-simplified. The British Consul-General's dispatch to his embassy in St Petersburg, for example, explained how the riots began when "an uncontrolled mob of dock labourers, strikers, loafers and all kinds of bad characters of both sexes began breaking open warehouses." The Reuter correspondent's cabled report of the following day placed the blame for the death and destruction equally on the military and 'the incendiary mob'. The official Russian report naturally tended to give emphasis to the political origins of the riots.

The real causes were cumulative, and the origins went back to the working and living conditions, wages, unemployment caused by the series of debacles in the

Far East, the crudely authoritarian nature of the government and the disaffection that had grown over the years to such a scale that it could seek expression only in violence. In the midst of the general strike and the mass demonstrations, two events within a few hours of one another then occurred to complicate the pattern and draw the tense strands between the authorities and their forces on one side, and the working population and the policitcal parties on the other, beyond breaking point.

First there was the arrival of the *Potemkin*; next the massacre in the afternoon: one to add strength and confidence, the other to add bitter hatred and the urge for revenge, to the revoluntionary cause. By the evening, even the strike leaders and political agitators had lost control, and the scattered groups that still roamed the streets were in a desperate and dangerous mood. Down on the Androsovski and Platonovski piers the first warehouses were broken open, and looting on a small scale took place. In Catherine Square, close to the monument of the Empress, a bomb was thrown from the front of a line of demonstrators marching towards a small detachment of Cossacks, killing several and wounding others. The answering fire of the Cossacks killed five and wounded another eighteen demonstrators. Incidents like these soon became more frequent, and by five o'clock, when an announcement of Voyennoye Polozhenie (or state of siege) was made, the sound of gunfire from one part or another of the city had become almost continuous.

At this critical point, with the first reports of looting arriving at his headquarters, General Kokhanov played his last card. Minor pogroms had been a commonplace in Odessa for many years past, and this was not to be the only occasion in Russia when the authorities divided the enemy against themselves by initiating a pogrom at a critical time. But never before can the plans have been laid so carefully or on such a scale. Within minutes of receiving their orders, Kokhanov's agents were at work in their own areas, inciting those already in the streets to attack Jews and Jewish property all over the city.

It was not a difficult movement to instigate. There already existed a strong anti-Jewish element. Most of the shopkeepers and all the moneylenders and many of the factory owners and richest people were Jewish. The intelligentsia was almost wholly Jewish, including an influential group among the university students, from which the political leaders and agitators were mostly drawn. A great many people already believed that their present situation could be traced to the cunning, clever, trouble-making Jews as much as to the Tsarist régime and the capitalists. It was a simple task under the explosive atmosphere to suggest that it was the Jews who had brought about this crisis, that every bomb explosion* and every pistol shot was Jewish-inspired.

The first acts of violence in the pogrom occurred while the most desperate of the demonstrators who had survived the Richelieu Steps massacre were seeking out and deliberately attacking parties of police and Cossacks, and as looting began on a serious scale in the dock area. By the time darkness fell, and Constantine Feldmann was beginning his two-hour harangue on the *Potemkin's* gun deck, many Jews, workers, looters, police, soldiers and Cossacks had already died, and the first warehouse was ablaze. Confusion, chaos and terror became absolute when several bonded warehouses were broken open, and barrels of liquor and wine rolled into the streets, to be seized by looting crowds already carrying away rolled

---

* Our man in Odessa was certainly persuaded of the truth of this belief. "All persons implicated in bomb-crimes and in attempts on the lives of the police are Jews," ran his dispatch. "This is so much taken as understood that there will be no matter for surprise if a very serious anti-Jewish riot presently followed . . ."

lengths of cotton, bags of sugar and food of all kinds, and every sort of manfactured produce on which they had been able to lay their hands. Fighting soon became general, Christian against Jew, Cossack against worker, rabble-rouser against gendarme, and murder became motiveless among the drunken crowds lurching through the narrow dockland streets and between the warehouses by the light of the burning buildings. Many held up the fire engines and turned them on their sides to form barricades; others died in the fires of their own making. "The wharves and warehouses of the port of Odessa have been burning since 10 o'clock," *The Times* reported. "The mob has carried off the merchandise, and the losses are estimated at many millions of roubles. The city is enveloped in a thick cloud of smoke . . . It may fairly be said that the mob have destroyed the entire harbour . . . The streets are strewn with killed and wounded, the quays are blinding walls of fire, and there is no quarter of the city which has escaped bloodshed and devastation. Firing continues in all directions, and everything in the port that will burn is being destroyed. . . ."

General Kokhanov now had substantial reinforcements in the form of a battalion of the 34th and 52nd Brigades, and the 23rd Dragoon Regiment from Tiraspol. He sent them out into the fire-lit night with orders to contain the riots within the dock area and to shoot all looters. For the purpose of this exercise, everyone in the dock area could be considered as a looter or an incendiarist. The soldiers, equipped with rifles and machine-guns, went out to do their duty. At first they showed a marked reluctance to fire on crowds which included many women and even some children. But when they were met by violence, and even bullets, they retaliated at once. Those who survived described how machine-gunners poured their fire into advancing masses of workers, or caught them in bursts as they poured from burning buildings. Even the British Consul, who concluded his report on the night's events with praise for the soldiery, who "behaved very well under very trying circumstances", gave a horrifying picture of the crowds attempting to escape from the docks' area, when "every now and then a rush would be made up one of the slopes leading out of the port, and the firing would be redoubled, killing men in masses. An incessant fire was maintained until after broad daylight."

By dawn roughly a quarter of the total area of the city was either still blazing or in smoking ruins. The port railway station, the adjoining warehouses and lodgings, all the warehouses on the Androsovski and Platonovski quays, the harbourmaster's offices, a long stretch of the overhead railway together with about a hundred wagons on it, were all destroyed. The huge warehouses of the Russia Company and the Kohkin Company were gutted, and open sheds containing stacked timber and stores of other non-perishable goods burnt to the ground. In the harbour itself, the skeleton remains of seven Russian steamers and a dozen barges still smoked. "The whole area is ringed with great flames as far as the eye can reach," cabled the *Daily Mail's* correspondent, who went on to describe the appalling difficulties of the ambulance and Red Cross parties who struggled through the ruins in search of the wounded, while marauding bands of Cossacks, their faces and uniforms stained black by the smoke, continued to pick off stragglers from the ruins and others who had come to search for friends and relatives.

According to the official report, a doctor said that all the bodies he saw were full of alcohol; and alcoholism and bolshevism were in fact to vie with one another as the prime justifications for the huge massacre. No doubt there was a great deal of debauchery among certain classes of the people on the night of June 28–29 in Odessa; but then everything occurred on an extreme scale—the fear, the avarice, the cruelty, and the lust to destroy, to kill and to avenge were all at a high pitch—and there were many hundreds among those whose corpses were carried away from the rubble in carts during the days and weeks following the event, who were innocent or curious, or who were only attempting to escape from the holocaust.

* * * *

The question of the funeral of Gregori Vakulinchuk was giving the mutineers serious concern. They had hoped to be able to bury their comrade on their first day at Odessa, after a full ceremonial procession through the city, but troubles ashore had made this impossible. By the morning of June 29 it had become urgently necessary to arrange for his burial, not only because the high day-time temperatures in the Black Sea at this time of the year made it hygienically desirable, but also because of the trouble the body was causing ashore.

Dr Golenko felt particularly strongly about this. "We can't let people go on being killed for the sake of a dead man," he told the People's Committee indignantly. "We must bury him and make an end of it. If no one will go with me, I am going alone." Many of those in the admiral's stateroom who listened to these words were forced to agree. From the ship's rails at dawn they had all seen that the very shape of the city had changed over-night. The level of the skyline had been reduced, prominent landmarks had disappeared, and between gaps in the smoke clouds it was sometimes possible to see acres of flattened ruins. No one could pin the entire blame for this huge disaster on the presence of the body of poor Vakulinchuk; but neither could it be denied that

Vice-Admiral Chuknin,
Commander - in - Chief,
Black Sea Fleet

The officers and petty officers of the *Potemkin* photographed
before the mutiny. Captain Golikov is in the centre, Commander Giliarovsky on his right, Father Parmen on the extreme
left of the picture

The Richelieu Steps, Odessa, photographed in 1905. The statue of the Duc de Richelieu can be seen at the centre and top of the steps

Demonstrators marching through the streets of Odessa, June 28, 1905; and some of the dead being identified by relatives after the night-long massacre

Cossacks bivouacked in Cathedral Square, Odessa

(*above*) On board the *Potemkin* shortly after the mutineers had taken over the ship

(*below*) The bodies of some of the *Potemkin*'s officers lying in state in Odessa

Afanasy Matushenko, in white jumper. A photograph believed
to have been taken at Constanza

As the *Daily Mirror* shows in this cartoon, the Japanese must have derived some amusement from the Black Sea 'engagement' after annihilating the remainder of the Imperial Russian Navy at Tsu-Shima a month earlier

The crew of the *Potemkin* coming ashore at Constanza for the last time, heavily burdened with their possessions and loot from the battleship, which was scuttled soon after these photographs were taken

CONSTRUCT IA PORTULUI CONST

it was a large contributory cause. The massacre on the steps would not have occurred but for the presence of the bier, and already that morning news had been received from a boat-load of workers that one of the fiercest and bloodiest battles of the night had taken place around the corpse. All responsible members of the People's Committee agreed that there must be a meeting to decide on a course of action.

To save time, the meeting was kept to the committee level, and although it was an elaborate proceeding to convene, it was not long before the members had decided to send a deputation to ask the permission of General Kokhanov to bury Vakulinchuk that day. They would feel happier with the Military Governor's authority behind them, for the procession would then be protected from attack, and there would be no danger of the funeral being made the justification for a new massacre.

It was to be "volunteers only" on this dangerous mission, and among them was young Feldmann, who recognised that he "might be censured for taking part in such a risky enterprise when my presence on the ship was indispensable", but also felt that "we had to show the sailors that we were as ready in act as in word to lay down our lives for the cause". He took the precaution, however, of exchanging his civilian clothes for a sailor's uniform before embarking with three bluejackets, and Father Parmen, who was included as an additional safeguard against violent interference and to carry out a small service over the body.

After landing on the quayside (with some difficulty owing to the still active fires and piles of debris), the party was surprised to discover that neither the bier nor the body, nor even the little bowl of offerings alongside it, had been interfered with in the course of the fighting. The corpse, however, was in a sorry state of decomposition, accelerated by the heat of the fierce fires that had burnt close to it during the night. Father Parmen's service was a hurried one, and the four men hastened away along the quay and up the Richelieu Steps, at the head of which they were greeted by a strong contingent of soldiers who at once surrounded them with fixed bayonets.

Feldmann was convinced that his time had come, and his fears only increased when an officer led Father Parmen gently away by the arm as if he were some missionary miraculously returned by the savages he had failed to convert. "We will treat you with all reverence," he was quietly reassured before being taken in to see General Kokhanov in his headquaters. Meanwhile Feldmann and his two companions were led in from the Nikolaevsky Boulevard to the courtyard of the H.Q. and there kept waiting under a strong guard of Cossacks.

Firing still continued from distant parts of the city, and the Cossack guards at last unbent sufficiently to inform them that a regiment armed with mortars would be arriving from Kishinoff, and artillery and more troops from Nicolaiev, later that day. The outlook appeared bleak, and they all expected to be put up against a wall and shot at any moment.

But at last Father Parmen reappeared in the company of a colonel, who told them that they had permission to bury Vakulinchuk that night, at two a.m.

"At two in the morning!" Feldmann exclaimed. "Anyone would think he was a thief, burying him at that time of night."

"Well, that's your business," the colonel replied shortly. "Now you can clear off."

The party left without further delay. It had been a somewhat frightening and humiliating experience, and they had their only positive success on the way back to the quay where their boat was moored. Corpses still lay everywhere, in the gutters and on the pavements and roads, where they had been shot down in the night, and the first funeral processions were already taking place. They were fortunate enough to meet one of these down on the quay, and Feldmann intercepted the undertaker and ordered from him a coffin more suitable for Vakulinchuk's ceremonial procession than the service issue one in which he had been lying for the past thirty-six hours. It was of oak, with brass handles.

* * * *

At mid-day, soon after the return to the ship of Feldmann, the priest and the two sailors, the cry of alarm was again heard: "The Squadron! The Squadron's in sight". Those not on watch rushed up on deck to join the others at the rails, and reports every few seconds were loudly demanded of the look-outs above. "Where are they?" "How many?" "Is it the flagship?" A streak of smoke on the horizon was clearly visible to all.

This situation, of course, demanded an immediate meeting of the Committee, and the whistle summoning members to the stateroom was again sounded. Already it was known that the distant vessel was a unit of the fleet, for her flag had been clearly identified. What action should they take now? Go out to meet the squadron, with all guns firing? Or perhaps attempt to parley with the enemy first? Unfortunately Matushenko was absent ashore, making arrangements for the supply of rations to the naval guard which had again been set up over the body.

"Don't let's lose our heads," Kirill told the assembled members. "We must stand firmly at our posts and meet the enemy boldly and with dignity. Everything is on our side—right and truth, strength, and the people. Let us go forward to battle!"

"For freedom!" the Committee echoed.

But once again those who had been longing for battle and for an end to this period of uncertainty were to be disappointed. Even as the People's Committee broke up and made their way on to deck to bring the battleship to a state of readiness, the word reached them that there was only one vessel in sight, that it was heading for Nicolaiev and not for Odessa, and that it was in any case only the little training ship, the *Pruth*, twenty-five years old and of only 1,620 tons displacement.

* * * *

Matushenko came back to a ship suffering reaction from the recent excitement. But he was able to lift their spirits by reporting that he had succeeded where Feldmann's party had failed. The chief instigator of the mutiny had marched boldly to military headquarters and demanded to see General Kokhanov. He was denied an audience, but he did have an interview with a senior officer, persuaded him that it would be more diplomatic to meet the wishes of the mutineers, and was never threatened with arrest. The funeral would take place almost at once, at 2 o'clock, and twelve unarmed sailors would be permitted to act as pall-bearers.

"I have never seen such a solemn sight as the funeral of our dear comrade, or so many genuine tears as were shed over the body of the sailor," wrote Matushenko of the occasion. "When we left the boat and went on shore near the body of Vakulinchuk, there was a mass of people, just as on the previous day. Immediately several men lifted up the bier and the coffin, and the long procession marched through the town in the direction of the cemetery." In spite of the fact that several thousands of their own citizens had subsequently died in the cause of the revolution and the city was still in a state of utter confusion, Odessa did the martyr proud. The word had spread that there would be no military interference with the procession, and people from all classes lined the route along Preobrazhensky Street. Many more stood on the balconies above throwing flowers down on to the coffin and joined with the crowds in the cries of "Long live the *Potemkin!*"

Slowly the cortege moved north, headed by Father Parmen, still wearing a length of plaster on his nose where he had been struck during the mutiny, followed by the eight pall-bearers carrying the coffin draped with the flag of St Andrew (the Committee had perhaps considered it inadvisable to flaunt the Red Flag on this occasion), and covered by piled-up wreaths. Four more bluejackets as official mourners brought up the rear. "It was an occasion," *The Times* reported, "of a great popular demonstration."

At 5.30 the body was lowered into a grave in the military cemetery while Father Parmen conducted another short service, and then the procession slowly made its way back to the centre of the city. So far the police and the military had honoured Kokhanov's pledge and made no attempt to interfere with the proceedings, and it is possible that the sudden attack as the procession, headed by the *Potemkin's* contingent, neared Preobrazhensky Street again, was initiated by a junior officer. It was a simple ambush. There was no warning. Suddenly shots rang out from a side street and a number of civilians fell. None was armed even with sticks to reply, and the procession dispersed in an outraged, shouting panic, Father Parmen and the sailors among them.

The priest and nine of the *Potemkin's* sailors contrived to make their way back safely to the quay and embark on their boat. Three more were left behind, officially missing. No one ever discovered whether they were among those who died in that sudden unprovoked attack. But at seven thirty that evening, the whole city of Odessa heard a sound that had long been expected, with fear by some, with excitement by others. It was the sudden deep crash of a heavy gun firing, followed instantly by an echo that spread like a shock ripple across the bay.

CHAPTER VI

The Bombardment

FORTY-EIGHT hours after the death of their captain, the mood of the men of the *Potemkin* was as uncertain as it had been in the last moments before the mutiny: taut, fervent and susceptible. The conflicting tides of influence had washed over the uncommitted mass of the crew without respite, with many of the 'conductors' and long-service regulars who had been opposed to the revolt drawing them towards a policy of inaction and eventual capitulation; most of the Committee members recommending caution until the mutiny of the fleet at Sevastopol; the Social-Democratic caucus, led by Matushenko and Dymtchenko, working all the time towards an aggressive policy. Never had an electorate been subjected to such intensive campaigning, with the two lone civilian agitators ranging over the ship from stem to stern, from bridge to engine room, like a pair of professional orators hired by the extremists.

The pressure exerted on the crew by these different factions had not relaxed for one moment; when neither the People's Committee nor a full meeting was in session, groups gathered informally in all parts of the ship to listen and argue, and the topic of conversation was always the same, on watch, on the mess decks, or round the hammocks at night. Every man in the ship had been involved in a crime for which the penalty was death; this fact, and the inevitable fear that accompanied it, had seized their minds so that they could think of nothing else, and talk only of the direction their future could take.

This could not go on for much longer. The tension built up by the conflict would have to find release soon. There was a limit to the endurance of the men's nervous systems. Besides, all this talking was tiring, and both Feldmann and Kirill suspected that they were developing laryngitis.

At last an opportunity for decisive action occurred just before the funeral party left the *Potemkin* in the early afternoon, when an official military deputation came alongside to confirm arrangements and to give Father Parmen the *laissez passer* that would ensure the entourage its safe passage through the streets. "There's a big military conference taking place at the same time," one of the soldiers informed Matushenko. "It's a council meeting to decide what they're going to do about you. Why don't you drop a few shells on them?"

"Where is it being held?" Matushenko asked excitedly.

"In the theatre. All the senior officers are going to be there. This might be your chance. As soon as you've killed them off, we'll join you. You can be sure of that."

Matushenko thanked them for the information. Of course they were right. All they had lacked up to the present was a target. But now by wiping out the entire military leadership, they could force the capitulation of the city within a few minutes. Half a dozen well-placed 12-inch shells . . .

The whistles had sounded, and the People's Committee was already in session, when Father Parmen and the funeral party landed on the quay. Having seen them safely on their way, Matushenko returned to the *Potemkin*. The deputy chairman had made good progress, he discovered to his relief. Dymtchenko, strongly supported by Feldmann, had persuaded the majority of the Committee that this was their great opportunity. In a remarkably short space of time, an ultimatum was drawn up, the terms of which were not perhaps so drastic as the extremists would have liked, but represented a great advance on what they had achieved before.

The bombardment would take place that evening, to be preceded by three warning blanks. Shell fire would be directed only at the theatre, and after it was over a deputation would go ashore and demand the release of all political prisoners, an end to all military action against the workers, the withdrawal of troops from the city and the surrender of their arms. All that now remained was to settle a time. Immediately after the return of the funeral party, Matushenko suggested. And this final resolution also was passed.

But this question of bombarding the city was a very important one, a member of the conservative element in the Committee suddenly pointed out just before they were to close the meeting. "I feel we ought to discuss it with the whole ship's company and see what they have to say." All the procedural formalities of a democracy must be adhered to. It was useless for Feldmann or Matushenko to protest that the function of the People's Committee was to take decisions on behalf of the crew, and that it was essential to act immediately: in their present sensitive mood, it was obviously dangerous to risk flouting the will of the majority.

"Very well," Matushenko agreed reluctantly, "sound the call to assemble the crew on the quarterdeck and we'll see what they have to say."

*　　*　　*　　*

Father Parmen was conducting the service at the military cemetery when the seven hundred men of the *Potemkin* assembled aft to debate the proposed terms of the ultimatum to General Kokhanov, and their Committee's decision to bombard the city's theatre. "These mass assemblies made an interesting picture," wrote one eye-witness. "The front rows sat around as in an amphi-theatre, the next rows stood, and behind them others stood on raised supports. Sailors sat in careless attitudes on the huge turrets and monstrous barrels of the 12-inch guns. The scene was bright with the clean white shirts of the sailors. Their manly figures were breathing with health and vigour. All their faces were serious and thoughtful . . ." This was an occasion that certainly demanded the serious attention of all the crew. So far they had taken no aggressive action against the civil and military authorities, relying simply on the threat and potential destructive power of their weapons.

Feldmann was aware of the vital importance of this meeting. It was now over thirty hours since he had been unofficially accepted on the *Potemkin* as the representa-tive of the Social-Democrat Party and liaison officer with the revolutionary elements ashore. He had learnt a great deal about the true nature of the mutiny and the state of mind of the crew since he had stepped aboard in the first flush of enthusiasm and excitement. His confident belief that the revolution in Odessa was as good as over had been sadly short-lived. But in spite of his dis-appointment at discovering that the mutiny had been engineered by a small minority of the crew, and that the rest had acquiesced only because they were sick of their bad food and were unaccustomed to severe naval dis-cipline, Feldmann remained confident that the battle-ship could still act as the starting point, the vital gun platform, for the revolution that must soon sweep over the entire Empire. Certainly now, with the power of the military in the ascendant, the general strike in Odessa was doomed to failure unless the *Potemkin* showed her teeth; and Feldmann must have been conscious of this, and of the great burden of responsibility he carried, when he stood on the capstan before the seven hundred men to begin one of his marathon speeches.

"Comrades, you have passed the point of no return already," he began on a dramatic and intimidating note. "There is no turning back now, no hope of a pardon, no reconciliation with the government of the Tsar. Only your complete victory and the annihilation of the enemy can save you. It is war to the bitter end— and now is the time to strike, to get in the first blow while the enemy is still confused . . ." He continued in this strain for some time, always emphasising that they were doomed men, the whole crew, unless they could fight their way out. It was a cleverly composed speech in which Feldmann attempted to instill into his audience some of his own sense of urgency.

"Our enemy's leaders are gathered now in the theatre, we are told," Feldmann went on, "we shall never again have an opportunity like this. The soldiers have already told us that they will join the revolution if we first kill their generals. So what we must do is to open fire now, without wasting any more time . . ."

At this point, such was the enthusiasn that Feldmann had aroused, his audience broke out into cheers, and the student was confident that the issue was settled. But once again, as in the Committee meeting, a voice from the back spoke up to destroy all the advantage he had gained. "We can't fire on the town," the sailor shouted; and at once another cried out, "No, we can't shoot at our own people." And the chorus of protest grew until the quarterdeck was in a state of uproar, some still calling out for a bombardment, others fearful of the consequences and as strongly opposed to such a drastic act.

More than an hour after he had begun his speech, Feldmann climbed down from the capstan and listened in dismay to the violent dispute he had started. "You shouldn't have done that," Kirill told him. "You were much too abrupt. You should have worked up to the bombardment slowly." Feldmann had to confess that it had been unwise of him to put forward the plan for the bombardment; it would have been more judicious to leave this to Matushenko or to one of the Committee members. Already some voices were calling out above the confusion of shouted words, "Turn him off the ship!" "We don't want any landlubbers!"

But another faction was calling out for the 'captain' to speak. It was not the only time when the mutineers sought reassurance in crisis from the authority that had once governed their lives. But the officers seldom responded to the appeal, Lieutenant Alexeev in particular being a nervous, negative figure who endured the vicissitudes of the mutiny's aftermath as an obscure, shadowy form in the background of events; a sort of puppet commander who always failed to perform in spite of the untiring efforts of its manipulators.

The cries for a ruling from Alexeev grew in volume above all others. But the Lieutenant seemed disinclined to act as mediator, and it was Matushenko who stepped up, as he had before, to quell the discontent. The appearance of this dark, fiery little figure always succeeded in silencing the crew, and now, as the pandemonium died, he began by upbraiding them for dividing among themselves. "We must remain united, brothers, if we are to survive, and now here you are quarrelling so violently that you'll be starting a shooting match next. Haven't we suffered enough bloodshed from the tyrants who have ruled us for so long? Come, brothers, the working people of Russia are looking to us for salvation . . ."

Afanasy Matushenko might well have swung the balance of opinion in favour of violence by the power of his oratory alone, as he had before; but the matter was taken out of his hands when a member of the skeleton watch passed the news that the funeral party was approaching the ship, and that it appeared that three of its members were missing. Matushenko broke off at once when this information was passed to him, and ran to meet the priest and the sailors as they climbed aboard.

Three of their fellow sailors shot down, slain by the orders of the military. The amnesty agreement broken without warning. The solemn funeral procession of their martyr broken up. The terrible story of the ambush travelled swiftly among the assembled blue-jackets, gathering colour and indignation as it spread. The attack may have been no more than a brief skirmish compared with the bloody massacres of the previous night, but where the death of thousands of civilians had failed to arouse the crew of the *Potemkin*, the loss of three of their comrades galvanised them into instant action. For once, no meeting, no resolutions nor show-of-hands were needed. Nor were any orders necessary. The men went about their duties as if an enemy had been sighted, clearing the decks, battening down the hatches, turning on the hoses against fire risk, and going to their posts. Ammunition was hoisted up from the magazine, the muzzle covers removed from the guns, first aid parties took up station about the vessel, and Dr Golenko transferred to the *Viekha*, which he decided to convert to hospital use. The *Potemkin's* triple expansion engines slowly gathered momentum, and began to drive the great vessel forward into the harbour. Up on the bridge, Matushenko had given orders to the 'captain' to bring the ship to within a quarter mile of the quay to ensure accuracy, although the extreme range of her 12-inch guns was some twelve miles.

The sun was low over the buildings of the southern part of the city. To the north, a few fires were still blazing in the docks area, the westerly wind carrying the smoke away over the sea. It was clear to all those ashore who had seen the vessel move into the harbour that Odessa, which had already suffered such fearful damage from the military, from strikers, demonstrators, looters and incendiarists, was to suffer again from the broadsides of a great ironclad, this time perhaps to be mortally wounded.

In the *Potemkin* the excitement had become intense. They were committed now. Nothing could prevent the bombardment from taking place. It only remained to see which of their batteries would be the first to open fire. The big 12-inch turret guns, the 6-inch guns in barbettes, the 3-inch weapons, or even the quick-firers? All were loaded ready for the order to open fire.

Up on the bridge, Matushenko, Dymtchenko, Mikishkin, Feldmann, Kirill, Lieutenant Kovalenko and the captain stood beside the gun controller, Petty Officer Bedermeyer, who had the rangefinder trained on the city. Their target might be no more than a mile distant, but it was not easy to pick it out from the confusion of buildings, and their low situation, with the quay and the steep, garden-studded hillside beneath the Nikolaevsky Boulevard towering above them, did not make his task any easier. The *Potemkin's* guns would, in fact, be shooting uphill.

At seven-thirty, the first shot rang out, fired from a single 6-inch gun. It was a great moment. "Behind the smoke of the shot, just floating out," Feldmann wrote, "I seemed to see the red battalions of the army of the revolution, marching victoriously, ever farther and farther into the heart of Russia. Behind the crash of the first shell I seemed to hear the triumph and rejoicing of the conquering people." But it was only a blank, closely followed by two more. It had been decided to stick to the original arrangement of firing warning shots and it did not seem to occur to anyone that these would provide an equally effective warning to the senior officers at their conference.

Both General Kokhanov and the citizens of Odessa were given fifteen minutes in which to take shelter before the first live shell was fired, again from a single 6-inch gun. There was a sudden blinding muzzle flash, the crash and almost instantaneous echo from the buildings, and almost a hundredweight of high explosive whined over the rooftops, to explode out of sight of those on the bridge.

But the spotter above had seen the fall of shot. "Overshoot!" he called out. This meant, inevitably, that some other building had been struck, and perhaps innocent women and children blown to pieces. To the men on the bridge it was an unbearable thought. It had not occurred to any of them that they would miss, especially at this point-blank range. Petty Officer Bedermeyer made adjustments to his rangefinder. "Get it right this time," Matushenko told him sternly. "We must hit the theatre and nothing else, do you understand?"

The new range and bearing were transmitted to the 6-inch battery, and the order to fire was given. Again only one of the 6-inch guns opened up, its single round a faint echo of the thunderous broadside from all weapons that the battleship's crew, and those on the land, too, must have been expecting. The men on the bridge awaited the spotter's report anxiously.

"Overshoot!" he called out again after a few seconds.

How was it possible? The men on the bridge were appalled at this second miss. Two six-inch shells must have resulted in loss of life, and they had opened the bombardment to kill military officers, not defenceless civilians, who had suffered enough already. Hundreds might be killed if they fired a full broadside.

"Whatever's the matter?" Petty Officer Bedermeyer

was asked. "This is the worst shooting we've ever seen." In fact it was no more inaccurate than some of the naval shooting in the Far East against the Japanese. And Bedermeyer claimed to have good cause for the two misses. "It's no good asking me to find the target and aim properly without a good large-scale map," he told the anxious Committee members hovering behind him. And there was no one present to dispute his astonishing claim,* and to ask how guns were sighted and fired accurately in battle, at a distant enemy and perhaps in a rough sea. What did a torpedo quartermaster, a university student or an engineering officer know about such technical gunnery matters?

What those on the bridge did agree on at once was that the bombardment must cease, although they also resolved to attempt to procure such a map for future bombardments. It might well be useful. Meanwhile the People's Committee must be summoned to discuss the situation, and to select a deputation to carry to General Kokhanov a new ultimatum. The whistle calling together the members sounded all over the *Potemkin*, gunners slipped unused shells from breeches, the men were stood down, hatches were re-opened, and life returned to normal. The People's Committee remained in session for little longer than an hour, drawing up the new ultimatum. The rest of the crew had to agree among themselves that the bombardment had been rather a tame affair.

There was surprise ashore, too, at the bombardment's brevity. Where anxious citizens and enthusiastic agitators had made ready for a massive barrage that would bring the city's centres of administration to tumbling ruins, three blanks had been followed by a couple of shells,

---

* Petty Officer Bedermeyer may not have been so ignorant and simple as he seems. Instead of a prison sentence or the firing squad, he received a reward for his part in the mutiny.

the first which had taken part of the roof off a house in Nyesjenskaya Street, and the second had caused even more superficial damage to the façade of a lodginghouse. No one had been hurt.

* * * *

Late that evening, General Kokhanov's second-in-command, General Protopopov, agreed to receive a deputation of the *Potemkin's* mutineers at military H.Q.

"What have you come here for?" the general demanded of the deputation when the white flag had been laid on the ground in front of his chair.

"We have fired on the city today to show that we mean business," the leading sailor announced, "and to demonstrate that we can take decisive action against you whenever it suits us. We do not wish to cause unnecessary bloodshed, and we therefore invite the commander-in-chief to come to the *Potemkin* at once to hear our terms, or to send some officer with full authority to act on his behalf."

"And what happens if we prefer to disregard your demand?" asked the general.

"Then we shall feel free to take any action that we wish. Finally, if we are not back on board ourselves by ten o'clock, the bombardment will re-commence."

General Protopopov arose and made his way across the room towards a door. "Very well, I will report the situation to the commander-in-chief."

General Kokhanov had by then reinforced the strength of his troops up to a garrison of over 10,000 men, with many more on the way. Moreover, he now possessed heavy and light artillery, mortars and large numbers of heavy machine-guns. In the past twenty-four hours, he had wiped out, or suppressed, the revolutionary elements in the city; and the ordinary citizens were too fully occupied with counting and burying their dead to find time to demonstrate. There had been a moment of uneasiness when he heard that the *Potemkin* was entering the harbour, her decks cleared for action; but the bombardment had hardly been a sustained one, and the accuracy of the gunfire confirmed the truth of every artilleryman's opinion of naval shooting. It was hardly surprising that a month earlier Admiral Togo had sunk or captured almost the entire Far East squadron in a matter of hours. General Kokhanov in short, could feel that he was speaking to the 700 men of the *Potemkin* from a position of strength.

His message was brief and to the point. "The commander-in-chief does not wish to enter into negotiations with mutineers," General Protopopov announced on his return. "If you feel you must fire more shells at the homes of peaceful citizens, then God and the Tsar will be your judge. Now you will leave—no one will interfere with you."

*   *   *   *

At a late-night sitting of the People's Committee, the deputation's report of their reception at military H.Q. was received with indignation. "We'll show him," members threatened. "We'll really bombard the place properly tomorrow, and that'll make him change his tune." But there must have been uneasiness behind the bombast in the stateroom that night as the men's sense of omnipotence began to fade. Why didn't the squadron come? With the crews of another five battleships at their side, no power on earth could halt them. "If only the squadron would come, the general wouldn't dare talk to us like that any more," complained one sailor within hearing of Constantine Feldmann.

CHAPTER VII

The Engagement off Odessa

THE Black Sea Fleet had curious origins, and unique
functions. At the outbreak of the war with Japan in
1904, the Russian navy had ranked third in the
world, after the navies of Britain and France. This formidable fleet of battleships, armoured and light cruisers, destroyers and torpedo-boats, had been divided between the
Baltic, the Far East and the Black Sea, a division of forces
which was to prove a tremendous handicap in war,
for not only were the distances between the squadrons
immense, but Russia possessed no bases or even coaling
stations between Libau, Sevastopol and Port Arthur in
Manchuria. In a short war, therefore, Russia's naval
strength could be divided roughly by three; and she was
in effect a second rather than a first class naval power.

Throughout most of the nineteenth century, the
admiralty had maintained a small naval force in the
Black Sea but the absence of a powerful individual
squadron had been felt in the Crimean War, and even
more seriously in the Turkish War of 1877–8. The only
solution, it became clear, was to build up all three of
her squadrons to a sufficient strength to meet an enemy
at least on equal terms in any of these areas.

With Turkey as the most probable future foe, the
weak Black Sea Fleet became the most important of the
squadrons to be reinforced. At the same time, to lay
down a fleet of heavy ironclads exclusively for the Black
Sea was a wildly extravagant operation, for by the
Treaty of Berlin in 1878, all except Turkish warships were
prohibited from sailing through the Bosphorus. In spite

of this crippling handicap, which restricted the fleet to an inland sea of some seven hundred by three hundred miles, and its potential enemies to one power, the Admiralty in 1882 put in hand a large naval expansion programme exclusively for this squadron. The 10,000-ton battleships *Tchesme* and *Catherine II* were launched in 1886, the larger *Sinop* and *George the Conqueror* in 1887 and 1892, the *Twelve Apostles* and *Holy Trinity* in 1890, the *Rotislav* seven years later; and the largest and most powerful of them all, the *Potemkin*, in 1900.

It was a fleet that represented, at least on paper, the greatest concentration of naval strength in the world. All these armoured ships, except the *Rotislav*, were armed with 12-inch and 6-inch weapons. And like every other vessel built for the Imperial Russian navy, they all took an inordinately long time to construct, possessed major design and constructional faults, and by the time they joined the fleet, were obsolete in their weapons and machinery. Had they been put to the test of battle, it is doubtful if they would have fared against the Japanese any better than the warships of the Baltic and Far East fleets.

"The Russian navy," commented a contemporary authority,* "has not shown marked enterprise, produced great naval commanders, or proved conspicuous in seamanlike ability." Russia, unlike Britain, the United States or France, had no strong naval tradition or history; she had never been a seagoing nation, there was no natural enthusiasm for the sea, even in the merchant marine. The sailors of the Black Sea Fleet, like those of the Baltic and Far East Fleets, were almost entirely peasant conscripts of little or no education. "The Russian," wrote Fred Jane† two years before the

* George Sydenham Clarke: *Russia's Sea Power, Past and Present* (1898).
† F. T. Jane: *The Imperial Russian Navy* (1899).

Potemkin mutiny, "joins as a man of 21, and joins because he is told to, not because he wants to . . . Ivan is a big, strong, burly fellow with a sluggish good temper —like a big Newfoundland dog. He is simple and childish, and his intelligence is not high. He is amenable and willing, anxious to do his best and to find fun in his profession in his own melancholy way." Jane summed up succinctly: "Ivan realises that he *exists to be shot at*; Jack, that he exists *to shoot at others.*"

The officer material was hardly more favourable. Nepotism was rife at Sevastopol, and a junior officer had no hope of promotion without strong influence at the distant admiralty. Resignations in the years before the Japanese war had been heavy on all stations, due partly to the corrupt promotional machinery and partly to the low pay, which varied from £91 for a midshipman to £415 a year for a captain, from which there were heavy deductions. In the Black Sea Fleet officer morale had sunk so low that battleships with a complement of six or seven hundred men were down to fifteen commissioned officers, and in shore barracks it was not uncommon for a midshipman to be in sole charge of 350 men. As the fleet was only in commission for three months in the year, for reasons of economy, this sort of situation put an intolerable strain on junior officers. Discipline ashore was often lax and the men frequently out of control. "I felt as if I was coming into a cage of wild animals," one officer, commenting on a barrack inspection before the mutiny, was quoted by *The Times.*

It was with this material, and in this context, that members of the illegal Social-Democrat party began operations in 1903. At first their progress was slow, mainly because there was little interest, and their pamphlets were wasted among the illiterate majority. But subversive cells were patiently built up on every vessel, and a system of communication devised to

establish liaison. Then the revolutionary cause gained
great strength when the commander-in-chief, Admiral
Chukhnin, devised a new means of economy that would
also provide employment for his men, who were not
overworked during their long periods ashore. At Sevastopol and Nicolaiev he sacked a number of labourers in
the dockyards and replaced them with bluejackets. Not
only were the dockers incensed by this action, but those
who remained found themselves for the first time working shoulder to shoulder with men of the fleet, with
every opportunity to inculcate in them their own revolutionary fervour. Without this indoctrination, it is unlikely
that the Social-Democrat party could have planned
the mass mutiny for the summer of 1905.

But of course other events worked in their favour:
the appalling mismanagement of the war, the minor civil
uprisings all over the country, then the Winter Palace
massacre, the fall of Port Arthur and the destruction of
the Far East and later the Baltic Fleets. These events,
added to the disaffection of the whole nation and the
highly-organised state which the revolutionary cells had
built up in the fleet, made mutiny inevitable by June of
1905. It only remained to decide when and where it
should take place.

In the first week of June it was decided by the Social-
Democrat leaders from each ship that the uprising
would take place during the manoeuvres and gunnery
practice in Tendra Bay early in July. At a pre-arranged
time, the party members on each ship would break into
the officers' cabins while they were asleep, cut off the
epaulettes from their uniforms, take their weapons, and
lock them up. Presented with this *fait accompli* in the
morning, the leaders were confident that the rest of the
ships' crews would join them. It was to be as simple as
that. There was to be no bloodshed if this could be
avoided. There was very little personal animosity

against the officers in most ships, who were merely an unpleasant manifestation of the power of the government, and besides, violence would be likely to alienate the very crew members they hoped to convert to the cause.

At this time the battleship in the fleet most highly organised for mutiny was the *Catherine II*, the most loyal the *Potemkin*. The *Potemkin* had been a great disappointment. At the November, 1904, riots ashore, her crew had shown reactionary tendencies which had caused grave concern among the party leaders. The *Potemkin*, after all, was by far the most powerful single unit in the fleet, and, cleverly handled, could remain out of range of the other battleships and shell them at leisure with her modern guns. Afanasy Matushenko was told urgently to redouble his efforts to bring the crew up to the required revolutionary standards. Time was running out. It was, therefore, with considerable surprise that the headquarters staff of the Sevastopol Social-Democrat party received a request from Matushenko to anticipate the main mutiny by a few days. He told them that he was confident that he would receive the full support of the crew. He and his lieutenants had been working hard to obtain more converts, and there was no doubt that the *Potemkin* was not a happy ship. Everyone hated, in particular, Commander Giliarovsky. Alone at Tendra Bay, conditions would be ideal for an uprising, and when it was known in the rest of the fleet that even the temperate crew of the *Potemkin* had overthrown their officers, the main mutiny would be all the more decisive.

Matushenko was ordered to do nothing of the kind. The whole success of the fleet mutiny depended on unity and synchronised timing. He must await the arrival of the rest of the squadron, and the pre-arranged signal to strike at the agreed time.

It has never been made clear why Matushenko disobeyed orders and anticipated the mass mutiny by several

days. He was both vain and excitable; he might, therefore, have acted to prove his ability as a revolutionary
and the injustice of his vessel's reputation, or because
he was carried away by the occasion. Certainly the
incident of the high meat presented him with the perfect
ready-made situation from which to lead the crew to
violence; and he may have found the temptation
impossible to resist.

*   *   *   *

The cable carrying the news of the mutiny of the *Potemkin* had reached Sevastopol early on June 28, the morning
after her arrival at Odessa. Vice-Admiral Krieger,
deputising for the commander-in-chief, Admiral Chukhnin, who was in Moscow, at once ordered a conference
of all ships' commanders on board the flagship *Rotislav*.
Krieger had no reason to doubt the truth of the signal
from Odessa; and he had every reason to believe that a
mutiny throughout his fleet had been planned for the
near future. The *Potemkin* affair was only a foretaste of
what was to come.

The situation was crucial, and it was urgently necessary to take action against the *Potemkin*. If the uprising
on that battleship could be suppressed without delay, it
might still be possible to nip the major mutiny in the
bud. Krieger called for reports on the state of loyalty of
every ship under his command. These ranged from
excellent on the flagship, to poor on the *George the
Conqueror*, and to bad on the *Catherine II*, whose captain
reported that only that morning his crew had refused to
sing "God Save the Tsar" after the "Our Father" and
the "Hail Mary". Krieger decided that it would be
safer to leave the *Catherine II* behind in any offensive
operation.

It was two hours before the commanders dispersed to

their vessels, those of the *Holy Trinity*, *George the Conqueror* and *The Twelve Apostles* with orders to raise steam at once and sail for Odessa with the light cruiser *Kazarsky* and an escort of four torpedo-boats. Rear-Admiral Vishnevetsky, in command of this squadron, was to reconnoitre, recapture the *Potemkin* if circumstances were favourable, and rendezvous with the rest of the fleet in Tendra Bay in two days' time.

The news of the mutiny and the murder of the *Potemkin's* officers travelled rapidly to the lower decks of every vessel in the fleet, causing intense excitement. Everywhere there was speculation on whether it would force the revolutionary elements to show their hand and order a general uprising at once. Then there was the more fearful question whether they would be ordered to take action against the mutinous battleship, perhaps to fire on their fellow countrymen, and be fired on in return. The average seaman looked forward to the immediate future with fear and bewilderment.

The officers were equally nervous. The prospect of leading into battle men whose loyalty was doubtful against the most powerful battleship in the navy was an unpleasant one. "They were terribly uneasy," one sailor recounted later, "walking about in a dispirited manner and whispering together."

It was not until eleven o'clock that night, when the eight warships slipped out of Sevastopol harbour, their searchlights sweeping a path ahead, that it became clear at last that the Black Sea Fleet was committed to battle.

*   *   *   *

Again there was little sleep for the crew of the *Potemkin* on the night of June 29–30. After the bombardment and the return of the deputation from the military H.Q. ashore, the People's Committee remained in session until long after midnight, and in all parts of the vessel the discussion between groups of sailors continued into the small hours. Many of the men stretched out where they had been sitting on deck, falling asleep with the sound of argument continuing about them.

It was the nervous exhaustion in being a mutineer rather than the physical dangers that were taxing, and even the most ardent among them were finding the burden of frustration and uncertainty almost more than they could bear. Their leaders were, of course, most affected. Matushenko, who had had probably no more than five hours sleep since the uprising, was looking gaunt and ill, and even the tough Dymtchenko had lost some of his exuberance. Kirill, who had arrived on the vessel worn out, had never caught up on his sleep, and was losing his voice. Feldmann was so hoarse that he had been scarcely able to speak in the night sitting of the Committee.

A sense of total inadequacy had also taken a firm grip on the *Potemkin*, and the buoyancy and self-confidence of the first morning had been dissipated in the endless rounds of People's Committee meetings, executive sub-committee meetings, and mass gatherings of the crew. What, after all, had they achieved since the killing of their officers and the capture of the ironclad? The uprising in the city that their arrival had set off had been cruelly crushed with the loss of thousands of lives. Their bombardment had been ludicrously inaccurate and abortive. Even the martyr's funeral had been broken up, with the loss of three of their number. For two days and three nights, bathos, disappointment, and anti-climax had followed hard one behind the other, each darkened by the fear—which was never to leave them—of the shooting squad or transport to Siberia.

The *Potemkin's* state of morale, then, can fairly be described as near-neurotic at dawn on June 30 when her radio room suddenly began to pick up mysterious messages, the first they had heard since the mutiny. "Distinctly visible . . ." ". . . we are in touch with you by radio at a range of five . . ." ran the tantalisingly brief broken signals. The alert wireless telegraphist at once informed Matushenko of these calls. "They carried the call sign of the *Rotislav*," he added.

Matushenko had the rest of the Committee woken up, and within a few minutes they were all crowding into the wireless room, loudly speculating on what could have been "distinctly visible" to the flagship of the Black Sea Fleet, and what unit of measurement had been lost in the ether. All that could be known for certain was that at least two ships of the squadron were on their way, and that immediate measures must be taken to receive them.

Once more the stirring words of alarm "The Squadron! The Squadron's coming!" ran through the *Potemkin*, and the weary crew tumbled out of hammocks or raised themselves from the decks where they had lain in the warm night air. This time the excitement was greater than ever before. This could not be another false alarm, this time it was the real thing. Already Matushenko had commandeered the swift little steamer, the *Smely*, anchored near the battleship, and ordered her out of harbour to reconnoitre under the direction of a concealed naval crew. In the *Potemkin's* engine rooms the stokers were urgently building up steam pressure, Dr Golenko was organising first aid and stretcher parties about the ship, the decks were being cleared for action, the gunners running to their posts.

But even now, with the crisis so imminent, the fundamental uncertainty remained that the enemy might greet them either as heroes and comrades or with broadsides of shellfire, taking the edge off their resolution and clouding their excitement. This unhappy state of affairs, so distracting for fighting men steeling themselves for their first combat, continued for two hours, and it was not until the *Smely* returned to Odessa roadstead at nine o'clock that all their doubts were dispelled. She had sighted three battleships supported by light forces, she reported, leaving Tendra Island and clearly heading for Odessa. All the vessels were flying the flag of St Andrew.

Matushenko was neither surprised nor dismayed at this news. He had full confidence in the power of the *Potemkin* and in the strength of the subversive elements in the opposing vessels. If it came to a battle he thought it unlikely that the enemy would fight determinedly. All the advantages were on their side, and a careful plan of operations had been worked out to meet this eventuality. This was the real moment of decision, perhaps the turning point in the revolution. The future of Russia could depend on the events of the next hour. Already smoke had been sighted on the horizon, and the lookout was reporting three battleships hull down to the east.

Matushenko hurried up to the bridge to join Alexeev, Kovalenko, Dymtchenko, Kirill, Mikishkin and Feldmann. "They are the *George the Conqueror*, *The Twelve Apostles* and the *Holy Trinity*" he was told by a seaman. "And there seems to be a cruiser and some torpedoboats with them." He handed the telescope to Matushenko who took a brief glance at the dark shapes still on the horizon and at once turned to Alexeev. "Give the order to raise anchor," he told his captain. "We'll sail at once. We don't want to get trapped in the bay."

A few minutes later the great battleship was steaming out slowly between the harbour moles, the red battle flag which had been reserved for this occasion, flying from her forward military mast. The *Potemkin*, all fresh-painted from her overhaul, was a handsome and formidable ship with her well-balanced superstructure, her extended flying bridge forward, and her three squat, black-topped funnels; and she gave a fine impression of grace and power as she headed for the open sea. A cluster of flags fluttered from her yardarm carrying the simple ultimatum agreed on by the People's Committee: "Surrender or we will fire". The electrically operated fore and aft 12-inch turrets swung slowly on their mounts, and the barrels of the beam 6-inch guns turned until they were trained forward in the direction of the approaching squadron. The range was nine thousand metres.

The distance between Vishnevetsky's squadron and the *Potemkin* was down to less than four miles when the three loyal battleships began to manoeuvre, apparently switching from line ahead to line abreast formation.

"Now they're forming up for battle," a voice on the bridge announced with authority. "They must have seen our signal. They'll be opening fire in a minute."

Rear-Admiral Vishnevetsky had indeed seen the *Potemkin's* signal; but its uncompromising terms must have decided him to seek reinforcements and await the arrival of his senior officer, an action for which he was later to be severely reprimanded. His three battleships continued their evolution through 180 degrees, and sped away to the south at full speed, their screening torpedo-boats scurrying along at their sides. Seaman Koshuba of the *George the Conqueror* later reported that the officers of his ship "ran about in terror . . . and were continually running to the engine room pleading with the stokers to work up steam to its maximum and promising them payment from their own pockets." This was doubtless an exaggeration, but the advancing *Potemkin*, her decks cleared for action, manned by sailors who had thrown overboard or captured their officers, must certainly have caused a good deal of alarm. But the crisis was brief, for almost at once the rebel battleship also swung round and made off back to the security of her anchorage. There was to be no pursuit, at least for the present.

To the men of the *Potemkin*, as the battleship dropped anchor at the harbour mouth again, the action had been no abortive, indecisive affair. It had been total victory. The enemy had advanced to capture their ship and had replied to their threat with ignominious retreat. The sense of failure and frustration which so many of them had felt after the miserable farce of the bombardment the night before and the anxiety accompanying their departure to meet the squadron, gave way to a feeling of triumph and exultation. For the first time they felt that they had justified themselves, and the mutiny they had brought about. "We knew they would be back," one sailor recounted later, "and that this time we should have to face the guns of the whole fleet. But this did not worry us. We were all-powerful. We had nothing to fear."

*   *   *   *

Vice-Admiral Krieger had taken on board provisions for three days and sailed out of Sevastopol with his flagship *Rotislav* and the *Sinope*, with an accompanying torpedo-boat force, at six o'clock the previous evening. Vishnevetsky had been given orders to rendezvous with his senior officer off Tendra Island on the morning of June 30, and if the plan had been carried out according to schedule, the *Potemkin* should be there, too, recaptured and flying the flag of St Andrew, at the scene of her mutiny. The ringleaders would then be taken aboard the flagship, and the fleet would sail back to Sevastopol for the biggest court martial in the history of the Russian Navy. Krieger had every cause for confidence that the *Potemkin* would have given herself up without a fight. Messages from Odessa had told of her inaction and hesitancy since her arrival, of her feeble and inaccurate shooting, and the evidence that there were serious divisions among her crew. Only a determined and unified ship could brave the threat of Vishnevetsky's force.

At the appointed hour of 9 a.m., Krieger's force was hove to off the bleak, uninhabited island, and there was no sign either of Vishnevetsky or of the *Potemkin*. Nor did wireless calls demanding information on his position bring any answer. Krieger felt only mild alarm. His second-in-command might be having some difficulty in arranging to man the *Potemkin* and it would take time to get steam up and bring her from Odessa. But he kept an ear open for sounds of gunfire, and dispatched a scouting force in the direction of the city.

It was not until 11 o'clock that smoke was sighted from the west and the main force came into sight. The vessels were travelling fast, and within a few minutes the lookout reported that there were only three battleships, a cruiser and four torpedo-boats. It was clear either that Vishnevetsky had failed in his task, or that the *Potemkin* had fled before he had arrived. "All ships' commanders to report on the flagship at once," Krieger signalled, and within minutes of the reunion of the two squadrons, the sea was dotted with little steam launches all converging on the *Rotislav*.

This time the meeting was a brief one. After hearing Vishnevetsky's report, Krieger gave rapid instructions to his officers for the second attempt to recapture the *Potemkin*. This time they were not to allow themselves to be intimidated. Although combat was to be avoided if possible, decks were to be cleared and both main and secondary guns were to be loaded and kept trained on the insurgent battleship, and boarding parties were to be drawn up ready for instant use. The squadron was to sail in two columns, line abreast, the *Rotislav* leading one column, the *Holy Trinity* the other, the light cruiser scouting ahead, the torpedo-boats spread out in single line abreast at the rear of the columns. "The Tsar himself has ordered the elimination of this shameful blot on the honour of his fighting forces," Admiral Krieger informed his senior officers. "There must be no failure."

On that day the Tsar expected every loyal Russian sailor to do his duty; and with the odds at five-to-one, it seemed hardly possible that they could fail.

*   *   *   *

In the *Potemkin* the lookouts remained alert during the morning, while the gun crews were stood down and given time to rest and eat their mid-day dinner. It was a brilliantly clear morning, hot but with a fresh breeze that made it pleasant to lie out in the sun. There was an informal party on the quarterdeck, with singing and dancing to the music of a concertina. Everyone was in the best of spirits, and even the old salts and 'conductors' who had been spreading gloom and prophecies of disaster and the firing squad since the mutiny, seemed to be carried away by the spirit of confidence and gaiety.

The inevitable warning cry from the lookouts was heard at 12.15. Five battleships. Almost the entire Black Sea Fleet. And that meant, since the disaster at Tsu-Shima, the entire Russian Navy, with the exception of the *Catherine II*. There were some good-natured cracks about the absence of the *Catherine II* among the gun crews as they ran to their posts again. "I reckon they wouldn't trust her against us—they were always a good bunch in the *Catherine*," one sailor called out. "Bet they've done away with their bunch of bullies, too." The telegraph was put over to Full Ahead, and for the second time that morning the *Potemkin* steamed out to meet the enemy, with the N267 at her side.

Up on the bridge Matushenko, Dymtchenko, Feldmann and Kirill stood together discussing the situation.

The aggressive Feldmann was still regretting that they had not pursued Vishnevetsky earlier, believing that all three battleships would have mutinied and joined them if they had had the courage to give them a few rounds. The others were less confident. "This will decide things," Matushenko kept repeating passionately. At this moment, on the bridge of the battleship he had fought for and captured in the name of the working classes and was now sailing into battle against the servants of the Tsar, he must have looked the very epitome of a revolutionary leader; a figure fit for the decoration of any Marxist pamphlet.

The earlier encounter had been carried out in complete radio silence, but this time as the two forces closed to within seven miles of one another, the *Potemkin's* wireless picked up a signal from the *Rotislav*. "Men of the Black Sea Fleet," ran the demand from Vice-Admiral Krieger, "I am appalled at your conduct. Surrender immediately."

Matushenko glanced at the message brought to him from the radio room. "Reply, 'The Squadron is to heave to at once and the commander-in-chief is to come aboard to arrange terms of capitulation. We guarantee his security.' "

*   *   *   *

The range was down to five miles, and details of the advancing ships were clearly visible, when Krieger's second order was received. "You do not understand what you are doing," ran the message. "Surrender immediately. Only by immediate capitulation will you be spared."

No advantage to either side seemed to be gained by this exchange of threats, but for good measure Matushenko repeated his earlier message, adding this time

that the *Potemkin* would open fire unless their demand
was met.

Krieger made no further reply, and now head-on
conflict appeared inevitable. It was possible to see with
the naked eye that the decks of every warship were
cleared for action, with the crews below or at their guns.
"The great fleet advanced on us swiftly and with relent-
less power across the calm blue waters," one sailor
remembered these last minutes. "It made a terrible
sight." Twenty 12-inch and four 10-inch guns against
the *Potemkin's* main armament of four 12-inch weapons:
five great ironclads; more battleships than Togo had
commanded at Tsu-Shima when he had pulverised
Rozhestvensky's armada.

In the *Potemkin* the range was being called out every
thirty seconds: "Five thousand metres, four thousand
metres, three thousand five hundred . . ." Matushenko
told the quartermaster to hold the same course, straight
between the two columns of advancing battleships. The
forward 12-inch turret was to follow round the starboard column, the aft turret the column to port. No
gun was to open fire without specific orders.

They were clear of the bay now, and the coastline
astern was a heavy smudged line without definition.
Ahead the fleet was less than a mile distant, and already
the light cruiser *Kazarsky* had sheered aside at the threat
of collision, leaving the *Potemkin* clear water ahead
between the columns of battleships, a five-hundred yards'
wide channel flanked by steel and an unbroken battery
of guns. It was the silence of those last moments that the
sailors of the *Potemkin* remembered most vividly afterwards, with no sound above the deep rhythmic thud of
the engines that accompanied them at all times at sea.

The absence of any life on the decks of the opposing
vessels added a further ominous touch of warlike reality.
Only on the *Rotislav* was a group of figures to be seen on

the bridge: Vice-Admiral Krieger, his chief-of-staff, the flagship's captain and second-in-command and several other officers, signalmen and the quartermaster, all clearly identifiable; and all of whom, according to several eye-witnesses, ducked rapidly out of sight when one of the *Potemkin's* 6-inch guns swung round until the barrel was aimed directly at them at point-blank range.

The *Potemkin* was abeam of the *Rotislav* and *Holy Trinity*, passing along their length at a combined speed of some twenty knots, so rapidly and at such close range that the 12-inch turrent guns had difficulty in following their target. She drove on between the columns at full speed, flaunting her red battle flag as a challenge to combat. But still there was no response, and it seemed as if the gunners on both sides had received similar orders to avoid opening fire first.

Only from the *George the Conqueor* did the *Potemkin* receive any sort of response. She was the third in Vishnevetsky's column, a twin-funnelled, single-masted, un-handsome battleship, and one of the most trouble-some units in Krieger's fleet. As the *Potemkin* came abeam of her the deck and turret hatches were thrown open as if at a pre-arranged signal, and great numbers of her crew poured on to deck, waving their caps and shouting greetings, "Hurrah for the *Potemkin*!" "Greetings to our comrades!" Before the *Potemkin* had passed her stern, the *George's* upper deck and quarterdeck were lined with cheering seamen.

"This was the moment we had been waiting for," Matushenko wrote later. "It was the beginning of the revolution. These cheers of welcome were spontaneous expressions of solidarity from men of the working classes who knew that the end of tyranny was near at hand. The Tsar's puppets had ordered us a welcome of shellfire, instead there were cheers." Already as the squadron slipped astern those standing on the *Potemkin's* bridge could see the crews of the other battleships emerging on to deck to add their cheers to those of the *George's* men. The engagement was over.

The movement that followed was as neatly and gracefully carried out as any *pas de deux*, as correct as any complex evolution created during fleet manoeuvres. The *Potemkin* made a wide turn through 180 degrees, scattering the torpedo-boats to right and to left as she did so, just as Krieger ordered the columns to reverse course and circle back towards her, so that the mutinous battleship now faced the same situation as before, with the two squadrons bearing down on her, this time from the west instead of the east. But now there was no longer any pretence of hostility between the two sides. Only on the *Rotislav* were the crew still at their stations, and they, it was learnt later, had secretly agreed between themselves not to open fire even if ordered to do so. On every other vessel the men had left their guns and duties below and were banked up in lines three or four deep, waving and shouting their greeting, so that this time as the *Potemkin* swept between the columns she might have been the Royal Yacht being received by the Royal Navy at Spithead. No longer did the gun barrels swing round threateningly; and the officers of the loyal vessels watched helplessly as the mutinous ironclad flying the red flag swept by.

On the *Potemkin's* bridge, Matushenko and the leading Committee members appeared to be emotionally carried away by this demonstration of solidarity. Only the realistic Feldmann watched the battleships carefully, keeping an especially cautious eye on the *Rotislav*. But unexpectedly it was the *George the Conqueror* that appeared to make the only hostile move, just as the *Potemkin* passed her port side to port side. Suddenly the great 10,000-ton vessel swung out of line away from them and turned in a full circle, putting on speed as she did so, and aimed her bows towards the *Potemkin*, evidently intent on ramming her amidships. She was flashing by semaphore as she raced towards the *Potemkin*: a last warning to surrender, perhaps? an order to heave to and await a boarding party? Only one man on the bridge could read the flashing dots and dashes, and the others all crowded round this signaller impatiently awaiting his transcription.

"The crew of the *George the Conqueror*," he enunciated slowly, "wish to join in your mutiny. Please come alongside." And in confirmation of the appeal, the *George* turned on to a parallel course with the *Potemkin* and eased her speed.

"What do you make of that?" Matushenko asked, turning to Feldmann. "It was a quick enough mutiny. And, do you see, the officers are still on the bridge."

"I don't know. But I think we ought to put on a boarding party and then sail off after the rest of the squadron before they reach Sevastopol. This might be the beginning of great things. But we've got to act at once."

Lieutenant Alexeev, surprisingly, had an opinion of his own on the situation. "It might be a trap, you know," he warned. "They could capture our boarding party and then steam alongside and torpedo us. I think we ought to wait until we've got their officers here as captives."

These words of caution, supported by the authority of commissioned rank, had a surprising and immediately sobering effect on the impulsive Matushenko. There had been no visible signs of a violent mutiny on the *George* he realised, and it looked as if there were still several officers on the ship's bridge. This was a moment for care. An argument broke out among the leading Committee members, with Kirill and Feldmann demanding action, and the rest in favour of keeping clear of the other vessel. The result was that, while a vociferous and unofficial sub-committee meeting took place on the *Potemkin's* bridge, the two battleships continued to sail towards Odessa at half speed on roughly parallel courses, but with the *George* nudging in towards the *Potemkin*, which as firmly rebuffed these advances and edged coyly away. Far away astern, and soon no more than smudges on the horizon, Krieger's remaining force raced towards the safety of Sevastopol at 15 knots.

"At least let's put a party aboard her," Feldmann said again, close to despair at the wrangling and indecision. "There's no telling what's going on in the ship and they may need all the help we can give them."

It was at once evident that the *George* was suffering from her own disagreements, too, for the lamp was flashing from the bridge again, signalling another appeal: "*George the Conqueror* to *Potemkin*, please send assistance."

Matushenko looked at this message and consulted briefly with Dymtchenko and Alexeev. "Tell the *George* to arrest their officers and send their delegates to us," he told the signaller, determined now not to take the smallest risk with his ship.

But the *George* would not be put off so easily, and as a final *cri de coeur* flashed back: "Things are going badly. There are serious divisions of opinion. We cannot cope with the situation ourselves. Send help at once."

This was all Feldmann needed to swing the balance of opinion. "We can't leave them in the lurch now," he said passionately. "For God's sake let's send some reinforcements."

The others at last agreed to this course, though still reluctantly and only on condition that a sharp watch was kept for treachery. So the steam launch was hoisted out and manned by an armed party that included Matushenko and Kirill. "Signal to us as soon as all the officers are under lock and key," Dymtchenko called to them as the little launch steamed away. "We'll keep some guns trained on her in case there's any nonsense." Feldmann, Dymtchenko and Alexeev, surrounded by a large and anxious group of sailors, watched the launch's progress from the spar deck, saw the party come alongside the *George* and climb up a rope ladder dropped over the side. A number of bluejackets were there on deck to meet them, and then they appeared to be hustled below.

Fifteen minutes passed, with the two battleships now hove to a half mile apart, and still there was no word or sign of activity. Feldmann could stand the uncertainty no longer and resolved to go with another party to find out for himself. His anxiety increased when, half way to the *George* in a whaler, they were intercepted by another boat carrying a written message from Matushenko. (Why should it be written down and then slowly rowed between the two ships? What was the matter with the radio, or the semaphore, or the signal lamp?)

"They won't make up their minds to arrest their officers," Feldmann read. "Come with an armed party at once." More than an hour had passed since the *George* had sheered out of line, making this surely the most leisurely mutiny in the history of maritime uprisings; and certainly contrasting with the savage spontaneity of the *Potemkin's* rebellion. But then everything about the *George's* behaviour seemed mysterious and irrational. A whole series of imagined situations—from orderly discussions of terms in the wardroom, to a prolonged shooting affray below decks—might have passed through Feldmann's mind as his eight oarsmen rowed strenuously towards the vessel.

The *Potemkin's* armed party shinned expertly up the ladder, rifles slung round their shoulders, with Feldmann following. "What's going on, and where are your officers? he demanded of the bluejackets awaiting him on deck.

"They're in the admiral's stateroom," he was told.

"Lead the way quickly," Feldmann demanded; and later described the events that followed: "As soon as we were near I commanded the guard to form. The sailors drew up in double file facing the stairs leading to the stateroom. 'March!' I commanded. There was hesitation among the sailors; they stood in silence without moving. I understood them. To meet the enemy face to face is not hard, but to be struck down from behind a corner— from ambush, not seeing who is firing on you, and without a chance of parrying his attack—was very difficult, and it made even the bravest heart hesitate."

However, after a few stirring words of encouragement, Feldmann led them on down the steps, revolver at the ready. Suddenly a figure darted out in front, and a familiar voice demanded to know where they were going. Fortunately for Kirill, he was recognised before a shot could be fired. "Where are you going?" he asked.

"We're going to arrest the officers," Feldmann told him when he had recovered.

"But they've been arrested already," Kirill answered in surprise. In fact, they had for some time been quietly packing their suitcases while Feldmann and his party had been "steeling our hearts to face death from the treacherous pistol-shots of the officers". These anti-climaxes had become a part of the daily life of the *Potemkin's* crew, who, even in their moments of greatest triumph, seemed doomed to ever-lasting bathos.

Matushenko later explained his reasons for sending his message appealing for reinforcements. The *George* had been in a state of confusion when the first party arrived, with loyal and insurrectionist groups in command of different parts of the ship and with no crew-member certain whether he was serving the Tsar or the revolutionary cause. A final order from Vice-Admiral Krieger, ordering the vessel to rejoin the fleet at once had been answered briefly, "Proceeding to Odessa for urgent repairs", which might have originated from the mutineers, or from the captain as a desperate face-saver. Certainly Captain Goosevitch still commanded his ships' bridge when Matushenko's party came aboard, although the engine room had ceased to take any notice of his orders long ago and he had been helpless to prevent the *George* from pulling out of line and pursuing the *Potemkin*. But, curiously enough, Matushenko saw no signs of violence; a sort of fluid *status quo* reigned over the vessel, with the captain seemingly practising discretion in remaining on his bridge, and the mutinous parties restricting their activities to oratory. Even the rounding-up of the officers was carried out peaceably, with no roughness on either side, although this did lead to the only shooting on the vessel. Standing, still immune, on the bridge, Lieutenant Grigorkov was less able than his captain beside him to bear the humiliation of the scene below, where the officers were ripping off their epaulettes and handing over their weapons. So Grigorkov stepped to the limit of the ship's flying bridge, drew his revolver, put it to his temple and, leaning far out over the side, pulled the trigger. After tumbling into the water below, his body drifted slowly astern. He was the only casualty.

Captain Goosevitch was later persuaded to join his officers in the steam launch, and with Matushenko himself at the helm, steering with one hand, a revolver in the other, they were taken to the *Potemkin* and locked up in the ship's cells. It was all over at last. The *George* was brought alongside the *Potemkin*, and the crews of both ironclads spontaneously dressed ship overall, waving caps, and cheering and shouting greetings.

It was a great moment when the two battleships, preceded by the little torpedo-boat, sailed into Odessa bay at quarter speed, past the outer mole, and dropped anchor in the roads. They had defied Vice-Admiral Krieger who had come to arrest them, and instead had captured from him one of his two largest ironclads. There could be no doubt now that they had the sympathy of the rest of the navy, too. It could be only a matter of time before they, too, overthrew their officers and joined them in the great crusade.

The leaders in the *Potemkin* had never been so confident of victory as they were on that afternoon. "Our minds were at ease," wrote Kirill, "and the constant nightmare of fear that the business would fail was replaced by a complete confidence in a rapid victory over our ancient enemy and the apostles of darkness and violence. Now we had our own revolutionary squadron . . . Tomorrow we would go to Odessa and take it, establish a free government, join the free soldiers, organise a people's army, march on Kiev, Kharkov and other towns, join the peasant masses in the villages . . . Then to Moscow and St Petersburg!"

CHAPTER VIII

An Undecided Crew

EVEN before the return of the *Potemkin*, the mutiny, on this, its fourth day, was having international repercussions. Shipping in the Black Sea had come to a standstill, and governments were making anxious enquiries through their ambassadors in St Petersburg about the safety of the lives and property of their citizens. Foreign consuls in their turn demanded reassurances of security from the city's prefect, M. Neidhart; who told the British consul-general, Smith, that two military guards would be posted outside all consulate buildings as protection against the mob. General Kokhanov also gave Smith permission to allow the five British ships in the harbour to move to the safer anchorage at Little Fountain a few miles up the coast, although "he could not answer for the pleasure of the *Potemkin*," and advised Smith "not to allow their masters to use their ships for political purposes or the distribution of political proclamations."

All this was changed with the news that the fleet had sailed. "I am sanguine but not certain that the Sevastopol Squadron is reliable and that it will deal with the *Potemkin*," Kokhanov reassured Consul-General Smith; and when the two battleships sailed into the roads so confident was he that the *George the Conqueror* had captured the *Potemkin* that he advised Smith, and the other consuls, and all the press correspondents* in the city

* The false news that the *Potemkin* Mutiny was crushed appeared in the newspapers of every European capital and the U.S.A. the next day.

that the mutiny was over. Several hours passed before reports reached him that in fact both ironclads were flying the red flag, and that it was the *Potemkin* which had brought the *George* under her allegiance.

"When it was found in the evening that the crew of the *George the Conqueror* had also mutinied," General Kokhanov wrote in his report, "and that the squadron had returned to Sevastopol without crushing the crew of the *Potemkin*, and even reinforcing them by a battleship, I had to reckon without the help of the Admiralty in my further actions, and to fight against the two battleships with my own forces alone."

This news that the revolutionary forces, far from being crushed, had doubled their strength, caused great consternation at military headquarters and near-panic among the civil authorities. The police and gendarmerie were warned that further disorders among the workers could be expected, and Kokhanov gave urgent orders to set up a battery of 9-inch mortars on Jevaka Hill overlooking the harbour and sent a telegram to the War Ministry begging for the immediate dispatch of long range heavy artillery. "The situation at Odessa," ran the report in *The Times*, "has changed with kaleidoscopic suddenness. The events which have occurred border on the domain of wonderland."

Admiral Chukhnin, who had left St Petersburg three days earlier when the news that the *Potemkin* was terrorising Odessa reached the Admiralty, arrived in Sevastopol to witness the return of what was left of his fleet. Of his seven first class ironclads, two had mutinied and another, the *Catherine II*, was so riddled with agitators that she could not be trusted even in harbour. First details from Krieger and Vishnevetsky of their disastrous operations off Odessa convinced him that two more of his vessels would throw in their lot with the revolutionaries at the first opportunity, and that even the crews of the two flagships would probably refuse to take aggressive action against the mutineers. Rather than risk the loss of further vessels and the lives of any more of his officers, Chukhnin therefore took the unprecedented step of sending the entire personnel of some 5,000 men home on indefinite leave, while a skeleton force of technicians visited the engine room of every vessel and uncoupled the bearings. For good measure, he also dismissed Krieger and Vishnevetsky from their commands. "The Black Sea Fleet," as *The Times* reported to its readers, "has virtually ceased to exist," and Chukhnin had to confess in a statement that, "I am afraid the sea is controlled by the rebels, and I have decided not to come out for the present."

There was talk of collecting at least the nucleus of a new fleet from the sailors of the Imperial Guard stationed in St Petersburg, who could reasonably be expected to remain loyal, but it would take a long time to transport them to Sevastopol and even longer to train them for their new specialist duties. The only chance of destroying or capturing the *Potemkin* appeared now to lie with the army; and Admiral Chukhnin was facing this humiliating prospect, when a group of officers asked for permission to see him.

These officers, some forty in all and drawn from the gunnery school and from several of the battleships that had returned to port, had decided among themselves that the honour of the Tsar and their service must be upheld, the deaths of their fellow officers avenged, and the *Potemkin* sunk or recaptured even at the cost of their own lives. They had, in fact, formed a secret squad which intended to seek out the *Potemkin* in a destroyer, close in regardless of the battleship's guns, and blow her out of the water with a salvo of torpedoes if she refused to surrender. This romantic and gallant group of aristos, led by a Lieutenant Yanovich, called themselves

the suicide squad; and all they now awaited was their
Commander-in-Chief's blessing.

Admiral Chukhnin warmly welcomed the plan and
offered the party one of the fleet's newest and fastest
destroyers, the *Stremitelny*, 26 knots, 220 tons.

At nightfall, and still in the greatest secrecy, the
destroyer left Sevastopol and set course east without lights ?
along the Crimean coast for Odessa. Unfortunately she
departed in such a hurry that the usual formalities were
dispensed with and her crew left the fleet identification
code book behind. They did not know of this at the
time, but its absence was to prove embarrassing later.

*   *   *   *

For Matushenko, Feldmann and the other leaders in the
Potemkin, the moment of triumphant rapture at their
new victory was brief. Feldmann, who had been left
behind in the *George*, was horrified at the weakness of
the revolutionary element among the crew. A small
handful of men had evidently taken advantage of the
demonstration of enthusiasm for the defiance of the fleet
by the *Potemkin* to take over control of the engine room
and reverse the course of the *George*. Most of the men
were terrified to find that they had been committed to
mutiny against their wishes, and, as Feldmann discovered, "instinctively tried to keep open a way of
retreat for themselves by laying the responsibility . . . on
the men of the *Potemkin*." They also showed the greatest
concern for the welfare of their officers and allowed Matushenko to take them away only with the greatest reluctance and on the understanding that they would not be
harmed.

To convert the *George*'s crew of six hundred men to
the Marxist cause was a formidable challenge even for the
tireless and dedicated Feldmann, now the only one of the

Potemkin's deputation left aboard. Like the *Potemkin*, the new recruit must have a People's Committee, and there must be meetings and propaganda speeches to instill some enthusiasm into the men. They must be made conscious of their responsibilities and prepared for their role in the revolution that lay ahead.

Feldmann threw himself into his one-man crusade with a will, in spite of his weariness and a voice that had now become so hoarse that it was acutely painful to address a large audience for more than a few minutes; undeterred by the rebuffs and occasional insults thrown at him, supported by only a handful of the ship's devoted Social-Democrat caucus. It was dusk by the time a meeting of the ship's company had been convened to elect the Committee, and even then this rapidly deteriorated into a general shouting match, with members refusing to stand after they had been elected and others having to be found to take their place. Many of these were 'conductors', and all seemed to Feldmann to be highly unsuitable for their historic role. He tried to intervene himself several times and induce in the meeting some of the *Potemkin's* standards of decorum; but his voice had lost its fine clear ring and was little better than a croak.

All at once Feldmann realised that he could not manage this tremendous task without help. The whole future of the revolution could depend on the state of mind of the *George's* crew on the following day; Feldmann had been told of the heavy troop concentrations in the city's dock area and along the sea front, of the new batteries hurriedly being dug in on the hills. Tomorrow would be crucial. The *George*, by turning neutral or re-asserting her loyalty, could destroy the cause within minutes.

After one final attempt at making a speech, Feldmann embarked late that evening for the *Potemkin* to report the state of affairs to Matushenko and the other Committee members. Night had now fallen, and as he was rowed across the stretch of water between the two vessels, he could see their searchlignt beams sweeping systematically to and fro over the waves: a pretty sight, "like careless water witches gaily sporting" as he described them, but also ominous evidence of their dangerous situation as rebels. "Things are critical," he reported when he arrived. "We must send more agitators to the *George* in the morning. If necessary we must make a landing and persuade some Party members ashore to come to our help." There was no lack of appreciation of the difficulties in the *George*, and Matushenko acknowledged the need for urgent action. But both he, Kirill and Dymtchenko were nearly as hoarse as Feldmann and were worn out from lack of sleep and the nervous tension of the past days and nights. Not for one moment had they been free from anxiety. Already that night there had been alarms. First a searchlight had picked out a dark shape heading towards them from the open sea, and the guns had been hastily manned. The vessel had been ordered to halt and had signalled that she had come to open negotiations on behalf of the Commander-in-Chief, but had shied hastily away when the N267 had approached to investigate. It was a large torpedo-boat or destroyer, the commander of the N267 had reported, although he had been unable positively to identify her.

Next came another form of 'attack'. One of the bridge searchlights picked out a sinister-looking object floating across the harbour in their direction. "A mine—look out, there's a mine coming!" came the cry of warning from the look-outs. The men sleeping around their guns woke up, alert for the new enemy, and a boat was launched in an effort to intercept it. But as it came nearer it was seen to be nothing more dangerous than a straw bale. "Laughing at the terror aroused by such a foolish thing," Feldmann described this midnight episode, "we went back to the ship, where the gunners stood ready at the first signal from us to fire along the beam thrown by the searchlight. Our news raised a laugh in the ship, too." Perhaps by now, though, there was a trace of hysteria in the mirth? It could have been forgiven.

*   *   *   *

The first occurrence at dawn on Saturday, July 1, seemed to bear out Feldmann's belief that the fifth day of the mutiny would mark its turning point. He had returned to the *George* with Kirill in the early hours to sleep in the admiral's stateroom (a revolver at his side) and awoke and went up on deck to find a number of the crew demanding to be set ashore. It was evident that the men of the *George* were more nervous and unsettled than ever, and that the loyalists had been busier than the insurgents during the night. Feldmann and Kirill conferred together in whispers, which by now was all they could manage anyway, and, recognising their own helplessness, hurried back to the *Potemkin* to seek aid. Matushenko had gone ashore, but Dymtchenko, Alexeev, Dr Golenko and the other senior Committee members were there and listened anxiously to their plea.

It was the most crucial Committee meeting of them all, and produced decisions at surprising speed. It was agreed that the situation demanded strong action, and that this time the persuasion of oratory would not be enough. A party must go, well armed and prepared to arrest the reactionary elements in the *George*, and hold the vessel until a contingent of orators could be procured from the city. Simultaneous meetings taking place in different parts of the battleship, it was thought, would soon swing opinion in favour of continued mutiny. And then they could all get on with the revolution. The only difficulty was the choice of leader. Dymtchenko, Kirill and Feldmann were all too stricken with laryngitis. Matushenko had still not returned from the city, and in fact there was now some anxiety about his safety. Mikishkin was too much of a dreamer. Nor were any of the other Committee members sufficiently forceful orators or bold leaders to take on this responsible task.

At this point in the discussion, Matushenko suddenly arrived back safely on board, bursting with his new plan to shell Kokhanov's headquarters. He had been encouraged in this idea by some soldiers he had met in the city, and had boldly marched along the Nikolaevsky Boulevard and made a drawing of the building that, according to Feldmann, was "wonderfully correct" and would guarantee an accurate bombardment. This time the gunlayers would have no excuse. In a hoarse, impatient whisper, Feldmann pointed out that they had a crisis on their hands and that "eager as we were to begin an attack on the town, we could not do so without making sure of the adherence of the *George*." Matushenko, deeply disappointed, had to accept the situation as it was, and that, as he wrote later, "we had made the great error of not having had the sense to rid ourselves . . . of the ship's petty officers . . . these corrupted and venal creatures." He had also to accept the fact that he was as unsuitable as any of the other three to lead the armed boarding party.

Suddenly, and to the surprise of the Committee, Dr Golenko spoke up and volunteered. He had taken no political part in events since the mutiny, confining his activities to the routine of tending the sick and to preparing for the reception of wounded from naval actions that had turned out abortive. Like Father Parmen's, his role had been a disinterested and merciful one, and he seemed hardly a suitable candidate. On the other hand, his officer rank* would add authority to his task, and it was this argument that decided the Committee to accept his offer. Fifteen minutes later, he was sitting at the bows of the *Potemkin's* steam launch, in the company of twenty well-armed sailors. It was the last the mutineers ever saw of him.

*　　*　　*　　*

The level of the *Potemkin's* bunkers had fallen dangerously low as a result of her two trips out of harbour at full speed, and Matushenko had made arrangements the previous evening to purchase from a wharfinger a barge-load of coal. The quantity was quite inadequate for their needs, but it would at least allow them some freedom of movement in any future crisis or action with the fleet. During the past two days it had become noticeably more difficult to obtain stores of any kind for the battleship. In contrast to the first day at Odessa, when boats of all kinds had come alongside, many loaded with food and clothing gifts for the men, the Committee was finding trouble in carrying on any sort of trade with the shore, and none of the little fishing luggers now came near the vessel. Although the crew knew that this change had been brought about by the repressive measures of the military and the police, it had nevertheless added to their unhappy feeling of isolation.

The coal had been a lucky find. Matushenko had asked to purchase it, but the barge-owner had told him he could have it with his blessings, so long as his vessel was returned undamaged. It was being hauled up and taken below in sacks and coal baskets, and the *Potemkin's* decks were covered with the heavy black dust that

* Although the *Potemkin's* three officers had lost their epaulettes, they retained their distinctive uniform and could not be confused with bluejackets.

accompanied every coaling operation, when the *George* hoisted a signal that caused the men to stop work and run to the rails in alarm.

"Am sailing for Sevastopol," it ran. "Invite crew of *Potemkin* to follow." In confirmation of this startling news, figures could be seen darting about the decks of the *George* engrossed in their tasks as if this were just another routine departure from port, and that it was evident that steam was being raised. There was no sign of Dr Golenko or of his armed party.

Matushenko raced up to the bridge, with Feldmann, Kirill, Alexeev and Dymtchenko behind him as soon as he heard the news, and precious time was lost in mutual disbelief and conjecture. It was too late to send another boarding party to the ironclad, for already they could hear her auxiliary engines at work on the capstans, and with the barge alongside and the other disruptions caused by coaling, the *Potemkin* was in a weak position to take emergency counter-measures.

But this sudden treachery had to be met with force, and Matushenko told Alexeev to have the decks cleared for action and steam to be raised. At once the alarm was sounded, and the gunners ran to their posts still in their coaling boiler suits. From the signal yard the pennants whipped out in the stiff breeze that had risen: "*George* remain at your anchorage."

But the *George* was already under way. Before her anchors were fully raised, she had begun to move in a wide circle that would take her past the *Potemkin*'s bows and out to the open sea beyond. Many of the mutineers left their posts in the excitement of this moment to shake their fists and shout angrily at the perfidious men of the *George* who had lifted up and then shattered their hopes so suddenly. Others came up to the bridge, and there was fear behind the appeals to their leaders to take action against the *George*. "We can't let them give the ship up like this," they called out to Matushenko. "They're betraying us—we've got to teach the cowards a lesson."

Matushenko had no intention of allowing the ironclad to escape, and as the *George* steamed slowly by he gave orders for battle flags to be raised and for the guns to be trained on her. At first there was no response, and then when the barrels of the great 12-inch weapons swung on to her at a range of a few hundred yards, her helm went over. "Another moment and another signal," Feldmann wrote of this moment, "and the *George* would be floundering under the fiery hail of our shells." Instead she showed her discretion with a signal of capitulation: "Am returning to my anchorage." "The feeling of power and victory," went on Feldmann, "shone in our faces, while the *George*, humbled and vanquished, passed again by the ship which she had meant to leave alone in the struggle with Tsarism."

With the counter-mutiny crushed, the surrender appeared to be complete and unity re-established. But Matushenko had under-estimated the cunning of the *George's* petty officers, and was taken off his guard when she sailed past the *Potemkin's* bows again in stately silence and continued on into the harbour. 10,000 tons of battleship heading for disaster at five knots: she was either out of control or a madman was at the helm. With the tide right out, she would be aground within seconds.

Strife-ridden since her departure, and as capricious as an over-indulged child, the *George the Conqueror* could hardly have chosen a more humiliating end to her disastrous voyage from Sevastopol. Still at unreduced speed, she drove her stem deep into a concealed mud bank, swung her stern slowly round under the impact and came to rest neatly, but at an unnatural angle, hard alongside the harbour's centre mole.

"Traitorous swine", "wolf", "criminal", "weak dog and devil" were some of the terms used by the mutineers to describe Dr Golenko, who had brought disaster to their cause when they were so close to ultimate triumph. The *Potemkin's* second surgeon was to become the subject of greater hatred and vituperation than any other figure in the 1905 revolution. It is possible that he was as weak and dissembling and treacherous as the *Potemkin's* crew made him out to be, and that he had remained in the vessel after the uprising only to await the opportunity of destroying their cause. It is also possible that his only concern since the murder of his fellow officers was to prevent the loss of more lives. Directly, and indirectly, Matushenko and his lieutenants had caused the violent death of some seven thousand people; and Golenko knew that the successful spread of the mutiny must lead to a real bombardment, and certainly to full-scale revolution in Southern Russia. Whether his motives were mainly political or humanitarian, he was well aware of the terrible consequences and loss of life, both directly and indirectly, a combined attack by the two battleships could cause.

Shortly after the *George's* grounding, and while the crew of the *Potemkin* was too distraught and indignant to take any positive counter-action against her, a distant group of figures was seen to be clambering on to the mole from the *George*, and then hastening away from her as if fearing pursuit. They were the unfortunate party who had accompanied Golenko on his armed escort, and with the military awaiting them at the shore end of the mole, the harbour water at the other, and the apparently hostile counter-revolutionaries in between, they were in an uncomfortable position. Luckily their predicament was recognised by the crew of the N267 lying alongside the *Potemkin*, and the torpedo-boat steamed rapidly to their rescue.

An account of the events on the *George* was given by these men, first to the excited and indignant sailors who received them on the torpedo-boat, and later when they were returned to the battleship, to the *Potemkin's* Committee. This is what had happened. The *George's* divided and anxious audience that gathered to hear Dr Golenko were told by him that the men of the *Potemkin* had decided that their cause was hopeless and that they would shortly be returning to Sevastopol to throw themselves on the mercy of the commander-in-chief. Golenko's recommendation to the mutineers of the *George*, therefore, was that they should follow their example. Nothing more could be achieved by continued resistance: the harbour was ringed with heavy artillery, there were thousands of troops waiting to repel any landing, and the citizens of Odessa were being evacuated in preparation for full-scale battle.

The doctor's escort had attempted to intervene and protest, but were shouted down and forcibly disarmed. Even the vessel's revolutionaries who had originally inspired the mutiny were helpless to intervene, and the *Potemkin's* sailors had, they said, been lucky to get off the vessel alive when she ran aground. There was apparently no chance at all of swinging opinion back in favour of continued defiance, and the *George's* petty officers had already decided to send forty men ashore to military headquarters to surrender as hostages, and with an appeal to the Tsar for forgiveness. It was all over.

This news spread rapidly among the weary, harassed and fretful sailors of the *Potemkin*, who gathered spontaneously on the quarterdeck, a milling, restless throng. The fear, the despair, and indecision so many had been privately nursing, at once found expression and produced a sudden unanimity of opinion. They would surrender. The responsibility for revolution was too much for them to carry alone. All the conflicts among the seven hundred men were suddenly dissolved in the cries of capitulation that arose from them, drowning the anxieties and frustrations of the past days. And so great was the relief from tension that the sound that echoed across the harbour carried with it a note almost of triumph.

It was not to their admiral, nor to General Kokhanov, nor to any Russian authorities that they would surrender, for from them they could expect no mercy; only the firing squad or the labour battalions. They would surrender to the nation from which they could expect a welcome, which possessed a degree of political freedom and had a strong Social-Democrat party which would be sure to help them. "To Roumania!" the men shouted in chorus, "Let's go to Roumania!" "We're off to Roumania!"

Neither Matushenko nor Dymtchenko nor any of the other members of the Committee tried to break up the unanimity of the sailors; indeed they, too, accepted the inevitable, and the hopeless task was left to Feldmann and Kirill. Feldmann, who had run down from the bridge in a state of great alarm, met some of the men on the spar deck and began to plead with them. "What do you think you're doing?" he cried out huskily. "Comrades, you're turning traitor to the revolution. Don't you see . . ."

But the sailors had lost all patience with this kind of talk, with insurrectionist oratory, and with the fiery, single-minded student in particular. Any notice taken of him was hostile, and for a brief, uncomfortable moment fists were raised and there were protests of: "Where do you think you're leading us?" "Do you want to see us drowned like sheep?" and even threats to hurl him overboard if he did not leave them alone.

It seemed to Feldmann and Kirill, who had worked so

strenuously for the cause for more than three days and nights aboard the *Potemkin*, that everything was now lost; that they had been called on to shoulder the entire responsibility for the great Russian revolution, and had keeled over under the burden. As the *Potemkin* raised anchor and left the half-wrecked city of Odessa and her stranded ex-confederate behind her, Feldmann could stand the grief and shame no longer. "In terror, pursued by phantoms," he remembered that moment, "I rushed to the wardroom. My mind worked in impotent misery and agitation. To surrender without a blow at the moment when we were ready for battle, possessed of gigantic strength—at the moment when all Russia was hanging on our decision—seemed a fearful, unbearable disgrace which could not be outlived."

*   *   *   *

The last smudge of the *Potemkin*'s coal smoke had scarcely dispersed on the horizon before another vessel steamed confidently into Odessa roads under the red flag. She was the *Pruth*, whose crew, encouraged by the success of the *Potemkin*'s revolt and news of her defiance of the entire Black Sea Fleet, had followed her example. The *Pruth*'s mutiny had been a replica on a smaller scale of the battleship's. On a cruise off Tendra Island, her trainee sailors had risen up and taken over the vessel in a brief fight which had caused the deaths of a midshipman, Nesterzev, and boatswain Kozlitin. But a few hours later, when the *Pruth*'s mutineers had dropped anchor off the harbour entrance, they found to their dismay that instead of joining a powerful squadron of two battleships, a torpedo boat and a fleet auxiliary, the city was firmly in the hands of the military, and that the harbour contained only a single crippled loyal ironclad and an abandoned auxiliary. The next day she hastened to

Sevastopol and surrendered in an attempt to redeem her defection.*

So as the *Potemkin* sailed south-west through the night at economical cruising speed to conserve her fuel, her crew were as alone as they had been immediately after the mutiny. But on that cruel, hot afternoon nearly a week earlier there had been triumph, confidence in the support of their comrades, and a sense of purpose to drive them on. Now there remained the uncertainty of their reception at the Roumanian port of Constanza. Only Kirill seemed to have any hope in the future. "Until we see that all is lost," he said in the wardroom that night, "we must live and struggle on." Feldmann was there to second the sentiment, but no one else. They were alone and, for a while, without an audience; for which, exhausted, depressed, and helpless with their laryngitis as they were, they may have been thankful.

* The price of redemption was high: four of her crew were shot, some forty imprisoned.

CHAPTER IX

Black Sea Cruise

THE crew of the *Potemkin's* first unanimous decision brought them only a brief release from anxiety and a few hours of peace from the speeches and rounds of meetings which had become an almost ceaseless and exhausting accompaniment to their duties since the mutiny. Self doubt came early after their departure, and Odessa was hardly out of sight before the battleship's sailors began to ask themselves whether they had not chosen the coward's way out, whether they were not betraying their comrades at Sevastopol who still might be planning to join them, whether in fact there would be real security for them in Roumania. On the forecastle, where for a time there was dancing and singing to the accordion, group discussions broke out, enlarged and became general. The familiar sound of argument was in the air.

In the admiral's stateroom, the People's Committee were hard at it again, too. Were the Roumanians to be trusted? What chance remained of other units of the Black Sea Fleet joining them in spite of the defection of the *George*? How far could they steam, and how long could they hope to live on their present stock of provisions?—and the answer to this was a few hundred miles and two or three days on bread, millet and water only.

It was Kirill who finally scotched the original plan to surrender to the Roumanian authorities. He had discovered in the captain's library a book of naval regulations which clearly stated that, under international law, deserters were invariably subject to extradition and return to their own country. This settled the argument. They would call at Constanza for coal, water and provisions only. There could be no difficulty about shopping there, for they still had plenty of money. And they could decide later where they would go after that; perhaps to the Caucasus, where, it was said, a peasants' revolt was going on. The *Potemkin* sailed on through a clear night and a calm sea, passing the port of Sulina at 6 a.m., without communicating with the shore. By four o'clock on the afternoon of July 2, the coast of Roumania was in sight.

Perhaps because they were anxious that their departure from Odessa might have been interpreted as an act of submission, the Committee was busy all morning drawing up yet another proclamation to the world, which opened, with characteristic grandiloquence, "Citizens of all lands and of all nationalities, the grand spectacle of a great war for freedom is taking place before your eyes." It was the crew of the *Potemkin*, continued the message, who had taken the first great step; and now they demanded of their tyrannous rulers the end of the war with Japan, and "The convocation of an International Constituent Assembly on the basis of universal, direct, equal and secret suffrage". For this they were prepared to perish with their ship, or conquer.

Perhaps to allay any fears that this threatening document might arouse, the Committee drew up another proclamation, addressed this time "To all European Monarchs", who were assured that "we guarantee absolute security to all foreign vessels navigating in the Black Sea and all foreign ports situated therein".

In spite of this reassurance, all foreign and Russian merchant vessels were confined to port. The *Potemkin* had the entire Black Sea to herself; nothing else was afloat on it, from Constantinople to Batum, except some anxious scouting warships of the Turkish and Bulgarian navies; and the destroyer *Stremitelny* which, failing to find the mutinous battleship at Odessa, was steaming south-west in rapid pursuit.

* * * *

The *Potemkin's* reception at Constanza was formal and cool; their stay marked by little episodes of frustration and comedy that had occurred so frequently since their mutiny. A launch flying the flag of the Roumanian navy and carrying two officers came out to meet them as soon as they had anchored, and was received with a courtesy salute of 31 guns. The officers were welcomed by a guard of honour drawn up at the head of the companionway and taken to the wardroom for a glass of vodka. They thought it might be possible to provide the battleship with coal and provisions, but the port officer would first have to receive the authority of the appropriate government department in Bucharest. They appreciated the urgency of the situation, gave Matushenko permission to purchase victuals for one day only and to keep the ship's searchlights on during the night.

Their next visitor was the captain of a Russian warship on a visit to the port, who arrived to pay the customary respects to his senior officer. Like the captain of the *Viekha* at Odessa, Commander Belavaniety was unaware that the *Potemkin* was in a state of mutiny (the local newspapers were full of it, but he could not read Roumanian), and was outraged to find himself being asked what he wanted by an officer who lacked badges of rank and did not reply to his salute. Kovalenko told him to clear off, and Matushenko, who had to be dis-suaded from violence because of the delicate diplomatic situation this would create, added confirmation that the *Potemkin* belonged now to the people, and when asked the whereabouts of his captain, indicated the bottom of the sea. Commander Belavaniety retired hastily to his own ship.

Their next visitors were from the Roumanian cruiser *Elisabeta*, who were more cordially received, and like their fellow countrymen, invited to take drinks in the wardroom.* Later Matushenko and Feldmann continued the social round with a visit to the cruiser, the officers of which warmly recommended them to surrender and promised that no harm would come to them. In fact, they were certain that the mutineers could at once take out naturalisation papers.

"And what about our ship? What do you suggest we should do with her?" Matushenko asked.

"Well, we could always buy her from you—privately, you know. The money would give you a start," it was suggested.

Matushenko, who confessed afterwards to being very offended by this idea, demanded testily the price the Roumanian navy would take for the *Elisabeta*; there were, after all, still plenty of roubles in the ship's safe. The conversation ended on this note of acerbity, and the visitors returned to their own ship.

After a night of strict vigilance in the *Potemkin* against attack from torpedo-boats and Commander Belavaniety's ship, the mutineers were informed that there would be neither provisions, water, nor coal for them, and that they would be well-advised to surrender at once. The People's Committee at once settled down to a long session in the stateroom, with charts of the Black Sea spread out on the table. The vexed question of where they should go now occupied the members for several hours, and it was one of the most heated meetings they had ever held. Alexeev favoured the little trading post of Eupatoria, Kirill wanted to go back to Odessa "where

* In contrast to their chronic shortage of food, there was always an embarrassment of liquors and wines of all kinds in the *Potemkin*.

the proletariat supported us so splendidly", others favoured the Gulf of Kertch, where the fleet normally carried out coaling. But Eupatoria traded in sheep, not coal; Odessa harbour would by now be sown with mines; the Gulf of Kertch had probably been closed to meet this eventuality.

Then Feldmann, who had been running his eyes down the pages of a *Guide to the Ports of the Black Sea*, took a sudden fancy to Theodosia. Colliers, it said, often put into Theodosia; and it had the added advantage of being *en route* to the Caucasus, where they had almost decided to start up a revolution anyway; although by now even the most ardent Marxists were concerned more with fresh meat and bread than any peasant uprising. But everyone was exhausted by the endless argument, and Theodosia was unanimously, and with relief, agreed upon as their new destination.

They were just about to leave Constanza when a telegram arrived from King Carol I, again begging them to surrender and promising that they would not be sent home. But the Committee was so disillusioned with a government that refused them even food, that had attempted to buy their battleship when they had refused to give it up, and had generally given the impression that they did not merit serious attention, that they raised anchor and left for their homeland without replying. Roumania had proved a great disappointment.

*   *   *   *

A state of crisis had developed along the length of the Black Sea's coastline. The *Potemkin's* crew's impression that they had been lightly brushed aside by the Roumanian authorities contradicted the agitation her arrival, with her demands, had caused in Constanza and Bucharest. This was a situation without precedent, and one that called for much research and deliberation at the Foreign Office. The Russian ambassador was emphatic: her crew must be interned, and the vessel handed over to the Black Sea Fleet at once. But according to one report, the Black Sea Fleet was in no condition to sail for Constanza, let alone take over a battleship that had already twice defied it; and according to another, and more exaggerated, report, the *Potemkin* had caused terrible damage when its demands had been refused and it had bombarded Odessa. To attempt to intern these apparently desperate men was clearly not without its hazards.

Turkey was undisguisedly indignant about the situation, and sent a stiff note to St Petersburg. Every vessel in the Turkish and Bulgarian navies was sent out on defensive patrols. Mines were laid outside important naval harbours. The gunners in the Bosphorus fortresses, now strengthened and ordered to remain especially vigilant, sighted in a searchlight beam a strange warship creeping up the channel without lights, and opened fire across her bows. But it was only the Russian Ambassador returning to Constantinople.

The Times, in a jocular reference to "the impotence of the Russian government at sea", commented on the Note that St Petersburg had dispatched to Bucharest and Constantinople with reference to the marauding *Potemkin*, "This document, we are told, calls upon the governments in question to treat the mutinous sailors of the Russian Fleet as common criminals, and warns them that should they act otherwise complications may follow. In other words, the Government of the Tsar is stooping to beg the Sultan of Turkey and the King of Roumania to be good enough to do for him the police work which he is no longer able to do for himself."

With the *Potemkin's* sudden departure from Constanza, even small coastwise shipping and fishing vessels remained in port. The mayors and prefects of every town and village on the coast had been informed by St Petersburg of the danger from the battleship, and warned not to give her any assistance; if the *Potemkin* persisted in her demands and threatened action, the population was to flee at once. Above all, she was not to be allowed to take on a single sackful of coal, for she was known to be as short of fuel as she was of provisions; and was not a hungry marauding beast the most dangerous of all?

* * * *

Having missed the battleship by twelve hours at Odessa, the officers of the *Stremitelny* scoured the Black Sea coast to the south-west, arriving at Constanza when the *Potemkin* was already half way to the Crimea. They could glean no information on her eventual destination from the port authorities, but, calculating that she might have cunningly doubled back to Odessa, Lieutenant Yanovich set a north-easterly course, and disappeared, still at full speed. At Odessa, if she failed to find her prey, she was at least able to express some of her vexation. Her victim was the little British merchantman the S.S. *Crawley*, discovered anchored in the roads compromisingly close to a mass of inflammatory political pamphlets washed upon the shore. Up dashed the *Stremitelny*, guns and torpedo-tubes ostentatiously manned, and circled round the unfortunate vessel, firing a shot across her bows. A search party was then sent aboard to discover further evidence, in spite of strong protestations of innocence; and, failing to find anything incriminating, returned to the destroyer which at once renewed the hunt and steamed off to the Crimea, leaving behind her a minor diplomatic fracas.

On refusing Matushenko's request for fresh water at Constanza, one of the port authorities had suggested that they should run the ship on salt water, as this would not do her great damage. "We've been doing that for four days already," Matushenko told him bitterly, "and we're getting hardly any pressure." On the voyage to the Crimea from the Roumanian coast, the engine-room staff found increasing difficulty in maintaining pressure in the ship's boilers, and the urgent necessity for stretching out their last coal reserves combined with the salting-up of the steam pipes, made their life a nightmare. It was as well that she had such a good start on the *Stremitelny* as the *Potemkin* was by now barely able to make half her normal maximum speed.

The men were little better off themselves. The ship's distillery was able to provide them with enough drinking water, but they had eaten no meat since their second day at Odessa, and their remaining supplies of flour and millet had to be carefully rationed out. The engine-room staff, and the stokers in particular, were most affected by the food shortage. "It was awful to see these harassed exhausted men," Feldmann told of an hour spent in the *Potemkin's* engine room. "I remember one of the machinists came up to me and, his voice broken and gasping with fatigue, told me that working in summertime in such heat, and on an empty stomach, was impossible. "We haven't the strength; our arms fall. Every moment you feel you will drop." "It needed all the self-sacrifice and devotion to the cause of these men to go on working in this hell."

But in spite of these handicaps and the increasing depression of her crew, the *Potemkin* looked as spruce and formidable as ever as she steamed into the little port of Theodosia at five in the morning on July 5. The petty officers had insisted on the maintenance of the navy's standards of cleanliness, and her decks and brasswork gleamed, and her guns would have done credit to the flagship during a Royal review. In addition, the People's Committee had cannily decided that because a fearful reputation was probably preceding them, every effort must be made to impress on the people of Theodosia, firstly that she was a happy ship, and secondly that she meant them no harm. To emphasise her cheerful friendliness they had ordered her dressed overall with her crew wearing fresh linen.

The steam launch was then lowered, and Matushenko, and Kirill, with an escort of two armed sailors, landed on the quay. They carried with them the usual proclamations composed by the Committee, the local one requesting food, water, coal and medical supplies, and the grandiose general proclamation addressed "to the World", announcing that they were at war with the tyrannous government of the Tsar and represented only the nucleus of a great new revolutionary movement. These were accepted at the Town Hall, with warm assurances that they would be passed on, and no one attempted to interfere when Kirill made a little speech to an unreceptive and predominantly bourgeois audience on the quay. The local gendarmerie and garrison of some six hundred military remained discreetly out of sight.

Later in the morning the Mayor of Theodosia, the Town Clerk and his assistant, and the town's doctor (badly needed since the departure of Dr Golenko) came out to visit the ship at Matushenko's request with a report on the supplies they could make available. Live and dead meat, engine oil, oakum, tobacco, matches, bread and flour, and some dainties for the sick, would all be supplied at once, the Mayor told them. But fresh water, a number of other minor items, and most important of all, coal, he could not let them have. He was a stoutly-built man, in contrast to his tall, angular Clerk, and clearly at the limit of his resources. One did not, after all, stand for election as Mayor in a small town like Theodosia with the expectation of having to face the might of a hostile battleship.

"Very well," Matushenko told him brusquely, "if you do not produce within twenty-four hours the coal and the water, besides all the other provisions, we shall blow your town to pieces. Now go back to your office and change your mind."

This was the worst that the Mayor had feared, and they all disembarked at once for a long session with the town's military governor. It was a trying dilemma. The *Potemkin's* 12-inch guns were less than a mile offshore, and were certainly capable of demolishing every building in the town in a short time. On the other hand, their orders from St Petersburg were explicit, and in fact a new decree made it a capital offence to give assistance of any kind to the mutinous crew. It was death either by naval gunfire, or the squad's rifle fire. That night notices went up all over the town ordering every man, woman and child to take to the hills as early as possible the following morning.

*   *   *   *

"An outstanding scene met our eyes at dawn next day," one of the *Potemkin's* crew remembered later. "Women and children, young and old, walked, dragging bags and wallets on their backs; rich people in carriages were driving quickly in the midst of a crowd that looked like an ant-hill. This sight set our hearts aching, in spite of ourselves, at the thought that all the pitiful possessions of these poor wretches might be destroyed that day."

Matushenko's ultimatum expired at ten o'clock in the morning, and shortly before this hour, the Mayor sent a message to the *Potemkin* assuring the crew that he was still trying to persuade the military governor to release the coal they required, and begging for an hour's stay of execution. Matushenko agreed to this and decided at the same time to go off on a tour in the launch with Feldmann to the inner harbour, which they had not yet explored. There they found to their delight a number of coal barges, all loaded and all unguarded. It appeared the simplest thing in the world to take possession of these, and thus to avoid altogether the unfortunate necessity of destroying the town.

Half an hour later, the launch again steamed away from the *Potemkin*, this time with an armed party of twenty-five sailors, headed by Matushenko, Feldmann, Mikishkin and Koshuba, and carrying the necessary towing gear. Matushenko brought the launch alongside the first of the barges, and remained on board with two more sailors, while the rest of the party clambered into the barge. They were making strenuous efforts to raise the barge's anchor when a company of soldiers suddenly appeared on the quay a hundred yards away, and without any warning opened up with a volley of shots.

The sailors were taken by surprise. Three fell dead instantly, and others were wounded. "Grab your rifles!" Mikishkin was heard to shout before the next volley, and the surviving sailors fell to the deck of the barge and began to return the fire. But they were exposed and hopelessly outnumbered. Several more fell into the water, where they were shot at again, while others leapt back on to the launch through a hail of bullets. But most were too late. In a sudden panic, someone had unhitched the launch from the barge, and she was already moving off, volley after volley slamming into her thin hull, killing a sailor called Tsirkounof and wounding in the stomach another named Koslenok.

Matushenko attempted to bring some sort of order to the situation and told the few unwounded men beside him to keep up a steady return fire so that the rest might be given a chance to escape from the barge. But almost at once as the launch got under way, a bullet struck and put out of action her steering gear, and she began to move around in a wide circle towards the quay and the bunched group of soldiers. "Seeing that everybody had lost their heads," Matushenko related, "that nobody had an idea left of how to behave, and not being able to get my comrades to act, or even to pick up the dead in the barge, I resolved to save at least the launch and what remained of the crew. Getting hold of the rudder itself, I somehow managed to get the head round and steer her towards the *Potemkin*. But all the way, for about a mile and a half, the bullets poured into us, several piercing the funnel and three of them grazing my cap."

A number of the less seriously wounded sailors left stranded on the barge dived into the water in a hopeless effort to swim after the fleeing launch. Among these was Mikishkin, who was at once lightly wounded by a bullet. Feldmann, who had miraculously escaped unscathed, jumped after him to give assistance to the injured man. Together the two swam with arms round each others' shoulders out towards the harbour, the bullets ripping into the water about them. Suddenly Feldmann felt his companion give a twitch, and then go limp in his arms. Seconds later the two separated, and the sailor disappeared beneath the surface.

Mikishkin had been killed by one of the last shots before the firing ceased, and the officer in command of the soldiers called out to the few survivors still vainly attempting the long swim all the way back to the *Potemkin*. "Come back and surrender," he shouted. But either they failed to hear the appeal, or preferred to risk death in the water rather than before the firing squad, and one by one they were picked off as the rifles reopened at them.

This sudden shooting affray, the loss of so many of

their comrades, and the failure of the poeple of Theodosia to respond to their arrival with any of the sympathy shown by the workers of Odessa, severed the last strands of determination of the *Potemkin's* mutineers. They might still be more powerful than any enemy they would ever meet, yet they were hungrier and more demoralised than any of the retreating armies in Manchuria, who could at least contemplate the luxury of a surrender at Mukden. With her unsurpassed batteries of heavy guns, the name *Potemkin* might be feared among the ruling classes of the whole Russian Empire, and in every land with interests in the Black Sea; and still the men who manned the great ironclad yearned now only for rest and food and security. They were too tired even to feel the shame of retreat from the rifles of a few soldiers, and the abandonment of their wounded shipmates ashore.

"Back to Roumania!" "Let's go to Constanza again!" rose the cries at the last mass meeting the sailors of the *Potemkin* held on the quarterdeck soon after the launch drew alongside and Matushenko and the wounded and dead were brought aboard. "It'll be better to die there or anywhere else than in front of a naval firing squad," one of the men shouted out when the alternative of surrender at Sevastopol was offered to them by Matushenko. They knew what would happen if they threw themselves on the mercy of Admiral Chukhnin from the fate of the ringleaders of the *George the Conqueror*, reported prominently in the local newspaper, copies of which had been brought aboard; none had escaped the firing squad.

It was a wan, dispirited meeting that contrasted sadly with those earlier occasions when voice rose above voice and even the conflicts added strength to the dominant note of vigorous optimism. Now they were conscious only of their abandonment, and their loneliness, and their physical hunger. Their impotence was represented by the huge 12-inch projectiles that lay neatly stacked, unused and disregarded, in the armour-protected magazine below decks; their final resignation by the little ceremony that took place far out to sea that evening when the big red battle flag was cast over the stern, "only the Black Sea witnessing our broken hearts and our tears," as Matushenko remembered the occasion.

For Afanasy Matushenko, who had worked for so long and with such devoted zeal for the mutiny, who had been more responsible than even Constantine Feldmann for supporting with his own strength the waning enthusiasm of many of the crew and stamping out the counter-revolutionary outbreaks, the men's decision to surrender to the Roumanian government was a shaming and terrible blow. And yet he knew that without the support of the rest of the fleet, whose crews were now scattered all over the Crimea, the Ukraine and Bessarabia, they could not go on; already hunger had so weakened them that some of the men could not carry out their duties properly, and in a naval engagement it was doubtful if they could defeat even a much weaker vessel. No, both the sailors of the Black Sea Fleet and the revolutionary parties ashore, had miserably failed them. Resignedly anticipating the reproaches that were certain to be poured on him, Matushenko demanded, "But is it our fault? Justice for justice, would we not be as reasonable as our accusers if we replied: 'Why were you sleeping, when for eleven days we were battling on the waters of the Black Sea? You knew well enough that one cannot drink salt water, nor make coal out of it. Why, then, did you not send us coal and water?' " But, of course, it was in the defection of the *George* that the cause of their ultimate failure lay; for if the two battleships had worked in harmony, destroyed General Kokhanov's headquarters, incited an army mutiny, and then sailed triumphantly to Sevastopol to take the rest of the fleet, there can have been no doubt that the fire of revolution

would have swept through all southern Russia. Matushenko might as well have reproached himself (and
Feldmann, Kirill and Dymtchenko) for succumbing to
laryngitis, and thus perhaps delaying the Russian
revolution by twelve years.

*　　　*　　　*　　　*

Just three hours after the *Potemkin* disappeared over the
horizon to the south, the *Stremitelny* sped into Theodosia
harbour, trailing a long white wake. She had scoured
every fishing port and inlet along the Crimea coast for
the battleship without success, and her crew of officers
were at their wits' end to know where else she could be.
They, too, were out of coal, and the engine-room staff
were concerned at the state of her engines, which had
been under a strain for which they had never been
designed for almost a week. Lieutenant Yanovich
found the town deserted of civilians, but he was at once
acquainted of the fact that the *Potemkin* had indeed
visited the port, and had not long gone. Once again the
Stremitelny rapidly took on seventy tons of coal and sped
off in pursuit, game to the last.

*　　　*　　　*　　　*

The *Potemkin* steamed slowly into Constanza harbour at
two o'clock on the morning of July 8, her searchlights
flicking to and fro to pick out the marker buoys, and
anchored in mid-channel. Matushenko at once went
ashore to consult with the town's military governor and
obtain confirmation that they could surrender under the
same terms that had been offered to them before. There
would be no difficulty about that, the general informed
them; in exchange for the *Potemkin*, the entire crew, if
they wished, could acquire Roumanian nationality, and

an assurance that they could live for as long as they wished in complete freedom in the kingdom.

Soon after daybreak, the men began to come ashore in relays in the ship's boats and her launch, many of them jubilant now in spite of their desperate hunger, and others loaded with linen, clothes, personal belongings and even some of the cabin furnishings of the officers. They were received on the dockside enthusiastically and as conquering heroes by the committee and members of the local Social-Democratic party, more formally by the civic authorities, who made temporary arrangements for their feeding and accommodation, and at Matushenko's request shared out the remaining 20,000 roubles (£2,000 approximately) equally among the crew. Later, the promised passports would be issued to them, and those who wished to remain in the country would be found work on the land or in factories.

Only fifteen petty officers and Lieutenant Alexeev refused the Roumanians' hospitality, claiming that they had been forced at pistol-point to remain in the *Potemkin*, and these men were given permission to leave for Sevastopol in the N267. Shortly before their departure, the battleship to which the torpedo boat had been a faithful satellite ever since the mutiny, began to settle in the shallow water of Constanza harbour. The *Potemkin's* sea cocks had been secretly opened at the orders of Matushenko by a devoted group of Committee members who were determined that their ship would never again become a unit of the Russian Imperial Navy. The great battleship's hull was lying on the bottom before the N267 was out of sight.

*   *   *   *

At the time of the *Potemkin's* surrender, Rear-Admiral Pisarevsty, acting under the orders of Admiral Chukhnin, was already at sea with his flagship, the *Sinop* and the *Holy Trinity*. He had managed to acquire from the Baltic Fleet nucleus crews believed to be sufficiently loyal for his purpose, and was searching the western part of the Black Sea for the mutinous vessel, which had been reported to have steered on a course for Roumania two days before. The Admiral arrived at Constanza just twenty-four hours too late.

*   *   *   *

The little *Stremitelny* heard the news of the *Potemkin's* surrender even later than Admiral Krieger. All through the night of July 7 she steamed south at her maximum speed and then north again towards the Crimea on a zig-zag course in search of her prey. She was close inshore, near Yalta, early the next morning when she sighted a vessel to the south. So far as the *Stremitelny's* commander was aware, his was the only other warship besides the *Potemkin* at sea, and he therefore had good reason for believing that his tireless persistence had been rewarded at last. This vessel was undoubtedly a warship and had three funnels of the same height and spacing as the battleship. Still at full speed, he altered course towards the ship and ordered the torpedo tubes to be swung out ready for attack. It was daylight, and besides her heavy guns, he knew the *Potemkin* was well-equipped with quick-firers especially designed to deal with torpedo-boat attack, and was accompanied by her own torpedo-boat. The odds were heavily against success, and the crew of officers must have known that few of them were likely to survive. But there was no turning back, for had they not sworn to destroy the mutinous battleship and avenge the deaths of their fellow officers?

In the imperfect visibility, the *Stremitelny* was not aware for some time that her target was only the old training ship *Pamiat Mercuria*. When the commander at last recognised her, he continued to approach the vessel in the hope that she might have news of the battleship, only to observe the *Pamiat* turn away as if in retreat and put on speed. The training ship's haste and nervousness were understandable, for she, in her turn, had not been informed of the *Stremitelny's* secret mission and believed that she was about to be blown up by the *Potemkin's* torpedo-boat, the only one known to be at sea. Nor could the *Pamiat* be expected to know that the *Stremitelny* had left her code book in harbour and was therefore unable to identify herself.

The *Pamiat Mercuria* attempted for some time to outpace the torpedo-boat, but in spite of all her efforts, the gap between the mutually suspicious vessels rapidly closed, until at last the *Stremitelny* was able to communicate by semaphore and ask permission for her commander to come aboard. When this was granted and identity established, Lieutenant Yanovich was rowed across in a whaler manned, to the astonishment of the sailors of the *Pamiat*, by a crew of officers in working dress and armed with revolvers. Within a few minutes the two commanders were able to explain their respective roles: the *Pamiat's* as a temporary hospital ship in the event that the *Sinop* and *Holy Trinity* forced the *Potemkin* to action; the *Stremitelny's* more desperate suicide mission.

Lieutenant Yanovich was anxious to continue the chase and prepared to disembark without further delay. But when he left the captain's cabin and came on deck again he saw to his dismay that his ship had suddenly disappeared behind a cloud of steam. Her boilers had finally succumbed to twelve days of extreme pressure and the tubes had exploded. The pursuit was over.

CHAPTER X

The Emigrants

THE Roumanian government remained loyal to their pledge to the mutineers, and St Petersburg, in spite of repeated demands, had to be satisfied with a sunken, but unsubmerged, battleship. It took two days' hard work for Rear-Admiral Pisarevsky's men to pump the thousand tons of water out of the *Potemkin's* hull and raise her again. Before she was towed away by the *Holy Trinity*, newspaper correspondents were invited on board to see for themselves the state in which the mutineers had left the ship, and as a witness to the anarchy and disorder which must have prevailed under the rule of the Bolsheviks. "I have just paid a visit to the surrendered battleship," telegraphed Reuter's correspondent, "where I found everything on the battleship in a state of wild disorder . . . The officers' cabins especially have been pillaged, everything worth taking having been removed. There are bloodstains everywhere."

The *Potemkin* sailed under tow finally on July 11, looking forlorn and neglected, and destined for a future that was to lack both redemption and distinction. On October 9, Tsar Nicholas decreed that the battleship's name be changed to *Pantelymon* (or "Low Peasant") as a mark of her disgrace. This however failed to raise the morale of her new crew, and later, when war threatened, she was re-christened more felicitously *Boretz za Svobodu*, a name meaning 'Fighter for Freedom', of which Matushenko and his lieutenants would have approved enthusiastically. After her two 6-inch wild overshoots at

Odessa, she never again fired a shot in anger; and, on completion of her uneventful war service in Sevastopol harbour, she was sunk by her officers on April 25, 1919. Like the mutineers fourteen years earlier they were just in time, for a few hours later the Bolsheviks took over the port.

When it came to the court martial of the captured or surrendered mutineers, the Tsar showed greater magnanimity than had been expected. After the court martial of the ringleaders from the *George the Conqueror* held while the *Potemkin* was still under the control of the mutineers and as a hasty act of revenge and example, the remainder were tried in the large military courtroom at Sevastopol docks on August 7. Among the accused were the petty officers who had escaped in the N267, Lieutenant Alexeev alone among them having persuaded the authorities that he was an innocent tool; the entire crew of the *Viekha*; and sixty more sailors from the *Potemkin* who had elected at the last moment to return to Sevastopol when Rear-Admiral Pisarevsky sailed in. The mass court martial proceedings lasted until September 9, when sentences of death were passed on only seven of the ringleaders, nineteen more being sent to penal servitude in Siberia and thirty-five to imprisonment for terms of up to twenty years. Among those who suffered the extreme penalty was Seaman Koshuba, who had been dragged wounded from the water of Theodosia harbour with Feldmann. The student was more fortunate. After a period in solitary confinement in the *Pruth*, which became a floating prison for all the mutineers, he was identified and transferred to a civil gaol, from which he succeeded in escaping, safely reaching the Austrian border.

After their first warm welcome at Constanza, the remaining six hundred mutineers from the *Potemkin* for a time continued to live satisfactorily and undisturbed in Roumania. All were found jobs, some in the Constanza shipyards and factories, but most on the land. A number of them married and had children and settled down. It seemed as if they would be quickly absorbed in the life of the country and that no more would be heard of them.

The first hint of trouble came with the Roumanian peasants' uprising in 1906, organised by the Social-Democrat party. The *Potemkin* survivors, with their revolutionary record, at once became suspect, and some eighty-five of them were imprisoned without trial for a period. After the revolt had been crushed, they all became marked men, and at times of domestic crisis, and particularly when prominent Russians or members of the Imperial Royal Family paid a visit to the country, were subject to police supervision and all manner of restrictions, which included a prohibition to change jobs or their place of residence. Several of the ex-sailors who flouted these regulations were deported to Russia, where they were tried and sent to labour battalions in Siberia. As time passed this tiny minority group found life more and more difficult. Nor was their position made easier by the behaviour of certain of their old shipmates who, according to one report* "soon discovered that the wages were lower than in Russia, that the food consisted almost solely of maize porridge, a dish as unpalatable to the Russian 'mujik' as it would be to the English agricultural labourer. Theft, insubordination, violence, and in one case at least, the murder of an overseer followed." The more stoic endured their handicaps courageously until, years later, the whole episode had been forgotten. Others sought their fortunes elsewhere. Matushenko himself, together with four of his friends, accepted the terms of an amnesty offered by the Russian government in 1907. Perhaps it was family ties, or the opportunity for continuing the revolutionary activity to which he had dedicated himself, which drew him back to his homeland.

* A correspondent in *The Times*, writing in September 1908.

But at the frontier he was taken into custody, and later hanged as a traitor. His companions were sent to Siberia.

Matushenko's right-hand man, Josef Dymtchenko, then thirty years old, fled Roumania in the summer of 1908, disillusioned and embittered by his treatment, still in search of the freedom and independence for which he had committed mutiny and murder three years before. With him were thirty-one companions, who travelled with their wives and children, and with their meagre savings had bought tickets that would take them as far as London. These refugees were for a time held at the German frontier at Ratibon as dispossessed persons, and at Hamburg the shipping company refused to carry them for fear of contravening the Aliens Act. But with the assistance of the German Social-Democrat party, they at last reached London via Flushing and Queensborough. There the British Friends of Russian Freedom took over, and an appeal was issued for funds to allow the ex-mutineers and their families to emigrate, by such prominent committee members of the society as George Macaulay Trevelyan, his brother Charles, Herbert Thompson, the Right Honourable R. Spence Watson and Arthur Ponsonby. It was stated that in South America there was "every prospect of their being able to obtain a decent livelihood, seeing that they were all vigorous and healthy, and used to work on the land."

The British Friends found the necessary funds for the party's passage, and did even better than that. They invited them all to a public meeting at 'Wonderland' in Whitechapel, where distinguished socialists made speeches, and Dymtchenko, with the aid of an interpretor, described the mutiny and its aftermath to the audience. Nor was that all. On the evening of September 16, "a meeting of a more convivial character was held in Whitechapel"; and songs in both Russian and English were sung. The next day they all sailed for the Argentine.